THE M

HEROINE'S

JOURNEY

OF

CONSCIOUSNESS

Molly McCord

The Modern Heroine's Journey of Consciousness
by Molly McCord
Copyright © 2013 Spirituality University Press
All rights reserved.

eISBN 978-0-9896045-2-9

Paperback ISBN 978-0-9896045-3-6

Cover design and interior formatting by Starfield Press
www.StarfieldPress.com

www.ConsciousCoolChic.com

THE MODERN

HEROINE'S

JOURNEY

OF

CONSCIOUSNESS

Molly McCord

DEDICATION

To every Modern Heroine
who is bravely answering
the Call of her Soul
and consciously following
the energy
of her dreams.

You've got this.

THE SOUL GROWTH ADVENTURE continues with *The Modern Heroine's Journey of Consciousness*, the second book in The Awakening Consciousness Series. This guidebook is designed to support you on your spiritual path by providing insights and definitions for your personal consideration and soul reflection. *The Art of Trapeze* is referenced as an ongoing example, but the driving intention is for you to consciously understand your own life experiences more. The main points from this book will be referenced in *The Unlimited Sparks of a Bonfire* – a travel adventure like nothing else!

"If you can see your path laid out in front of you step by step,
you know it's not your path.
Your own path you make with every step you take.
That's why it's your path."

~ **Joseph Campbell**

CONTENTS

INTRODUCTION

Everything these days is about "the journey." Ask any entrepreneur, life coach, author, artist, teacher, or traveler how many times they've heard that phrase, and if they don't roll their eyes, or cut you off mid-sentence with "I KNOW", or energetically flip you off, then consider yourself spared because on some level, she's probably reached a place of inner peace about the fact that she's on "a journey." Or else she was just ignoring you and then flipped you off when you turned your back.

Why has "the journey" become so popular in our modern lives? Why does it resonate with millions of people and easily relate to a variety of life circumstances? I believe the shorthand answer is because acknowledging that something is "a journey" offers the dual potentials of removing any fears about a present situation and adding more peace to potential outcomes.

Clients aren't showing up? "That's part of the journey." Not sure what to do next in your life? "Oh, a very valuable phase of the journey." Want to get started on a new professional direction, a new dream, a fresh project? "Oh, you're at the beginning of a journey!" Moving through a tough patch in your marriage? "Every relationship is a journey."

And really, it's true. "The journey" is an absolutely accurate and valid and appropriate descriptor of what we're all doing in our lives. We're journeying through lessons, relationships, goals, personal growth, and the supermarket. We're navigating and stumbling and learning and meditating as we go. We're living at a time in human history where we have more tools, resources, books, experts, classes, and free webinars than we know where to click a mouse at. And wherever you are on your journey, there's probably even an app for that, too.

Experiencing "the journey" is not a new concept. Raise your hand if you've heard of Joseph Campbell. He is still arguably one of the most influential people in the world on the topics of mythology, stories, and archetypes. For those who did not raise their hand, Mr. Campbell was a writer, lecturer, and professor known for his expertise in mythology, folklore, and comparative religion. Admired for his great depths of intelligence, storytelling, and insights, Campbell is also known for being the godfather of "the hero's journey" as described in his book, *The Hero With A Thousand*

Faces.

Campbell used the term "monomyth" to convey how, across multiple cultures and religions, the stories, adventures, and growth of the hero's journey are all connected to a similar pattern of growth. The archetypal hero's journey is recognized as holding common narrative elements, as Campbell references the 12 stages an archetypal hero goes through to obtain his ultimate goal, reward, and mastery. The 12 stages occur under three main segments: the Departure, when he leaves the known world; the Initiation, when he experiences trials, tribulations, and growth; and the Return, when he comes back to the world as a different version of himself.

Screenwriters study the 12 phases of the journey thoroughly for story development and guidance; editors look for it in published adventures, novels, and storytelling; artists reference it for creative inspiration. The archetypal hero's journey is well-documented in modern culture through some of the most popular films of our time, including the "Star Wars" movies, "The Lord of the Rings" trilogy, "The Matrix" series, and numerous Disney stories. Men becoming heroes is referenced continually because we *see* the journey physically, visually, unfolding in front of our eyes (and oh, what a surprise, it typically involves a sword/lightsaber/crazy-cool weapon).

But what about the ladies? Don't get me wrong, lightsabers ARE amazing for a solid three seconds.

Then I'm ready for another way to interpret a journey. After an extensive search that involved carefully typing "the heroine..." into Amazon's search box, I discovered a highly-revered book by Maureen Murdock called *The Heroine's Journey: Woman's Quest for Wholeness*. I ordered it, read it, resonated with it, loved it. Referencing mythology, goddesses, and gender, Murdock details ten stages of the feminine healing process that brings her back to her whole authentic energy as the goal, reward, and mastery. Her explanation of the journey starts with women identifying with the Masculine as their Father's Daughter, continues on to an urgent yearning to reconnect with the Feminine, then healing the Mother-Daughter split, and finally, whole integration of Masculine and Feminine energies.

Notably, Murdock had a personal conversation with Joseph Campbell about the differences between the hero's journey and the heroine's journey. One of Mr. Campbell's remarks was rather startling. "Women don't need to make the journey... because in the mythological tradition, the woman is *there*."

Say what, Joe?

With all due respect, Mr. Campbell, women don't live in the mindset of mythological times, and I doubt many of us assume we're already *there* in our lives. Granted, that quote was from 1981, and it is probably fair to say that maybe we *all* need forgiveness for something we said, or did, or wore in the 80's.

After examining both of these valuable contributions, I wasn't content leaving my understanding of "the journey" in terms of only gender. *What about spiritual growth? How are we able to expand our personal consciousness in modern times? How does the archetypal hero's journey relate to our crazy-hectic-busy lives, contemporary choices, and a quest for personal spiritual growth?*

I put these questions on the mental back burner and returned to my writing projects as obsessed, neurotic authors do. And then it slowly dawned on me that the answers were already right there in front of me. *Right there.* In the form of my own life choices. I had actually lived the archetypal journey not once, not twice, but *four* times to date, and I had no idea at the time it was *a thing.* You mean every time I went out on a grand life adventure, followed my heart and spiritually grew it was *a thing*? You mean all of the emotions and obstacles and growth and manifestations are *a thing?!* (You mean *I'm* Luke Skywalker in this version? Fist pump.) And it's all captured in my memoir *The Art of Trapeze: One Woman's Journey of Soaring, Surrendering, and Awakening*, which is written in alignment with the 12 stages of the hero's journey. I would love to tell you *I knew that* from the very beginning (really, I WOULD love to claim I had that trick up my sleeve), but it wouldn't be true. I simply wrote my journey as it transpired, and only in hindsight it became clear that I lived the hero's journey with my crazy-cool weapon of choice being three-inch high heels. Most importantly, this version of the journey is about spiritual growth and expanding consciousness.

Notably, the journey of spiritual growth is different from the visual, physical, public hero's journey we typically recognize in movies. Spiritual growth is a personal, internal, sacred, emotional experience often viewed only by invitation. It is different for every person and for each woman, yet there are also common themes and stages that make spiritual growth an archetypal journey.

At the risk of stating the obvious, this is where it is important to highlight that spiritual growth does not happen in the same way for everyone on the planet. (Just to cover ALL the bases with absolute clarity.) And it's even more crucial to state that it is not *supposed* to. There is no one set path, or "right way", or required formula to spiritually grow. You choose it for yourself. And a single "right way" wouldn't even be possible. Back in the 90's, I can remember having loooong discussions in undergraduate women's studies classes around the female story and the many variables of gender, race, age, culture, socioeconomic status and on, and on. As a political science major, I loved to throw in the dynamics of politics, power, status, access to power, and on and on. With deeper study into internationalism and diplomacy in graduate school, the human journey became even more varied with global perspectives, multiculturalism, religion, languages, geography, belief systems, political structures, and on and on. Eventually (and predictably), the conversation always arrives at the importance and validity of an individualized, personal journey. That is a certain conclusion for understanding a spiritual growth journey, too.

Remember, we're talking about an *archetype* of a journey. Campbell provides 12 stages of the hero's journey, but going through all stages is not the only way to experience a journey. And if you're wondering what an archetype is, think of chicken soup. There are essential ingredients needed to make chicken soup, right? You'll need chicken, broth, carrots, celery, any other vegetables you prefer, noodles, maybe some rice, and whatever secret ingredients excite you or your grandma. The archetype of chicken soup has key ingredients, but it can be made in various ways and still be called chicken soup. Equally important with an archetype is that it doesn't require all ingredients, or stages of the journey. You can skip a stage (no celery), overlap a few stages at once (use noodles and rice together), stay in one stage for a very long time (in the slow cooker), or choose to never move out of a stage because you prefer it the most (chicken soup for every meal!). Eventually, you have a journey (a bowl of chicken soup) that is uniquely yours, created to your own liking, and it has contributed to nourishing your spiritual growth. Multiple versions of an archetypal journey are necessary and needed, especially when the possibilities for contemporary spiritual growth are limitless. Plus, the journey is your Soul's unique energy that couldn't even be duplicated, or copied, or repeated by another.

This brings us to another important question: *Who is today's modern heroine?* I refer to the *archetype* of a modern heroine as a Trapeze Artist. A Trapeze Artist is a woman who jumps for any number of dreams in her life, from world travel and life adventures, to owning her own business, expressing her creative skills, or completing a marathon. She volunteers in the Peace Corps, or decides to leave a job to raise her children, or goes back to an office after raising children. She has battled through extreme weight loss, or bravely opened up to her true sexuality and owns it. She has served in the military and returned home as a different woman. Or she has entered a national televised singing competition and experienced an extreme life transformation.

A Trapeze Artist is any woman who has taken a huge leap of faith and trusted beyond what she could see, or prove, or touch. She chose to trust within; to believe in her power. She is open to expanding beyond any limiting self-definition that has kept her unconsciously small in her life, her energy, her dreams. She is actively practicing self-trust, activating deeper levels of faith, and powerfully creating her vision. She is a woman who honors her emotional process and accepts all parts of herself with unconditional love, claiming her own Divinity as a birthright and a gift. And she knows when it is time to surrender to something bigger than herself.

A Trapeze Artist is soaring from the Unconscious part of her existence into fully awakened Consciousness where she claims the most of her Soul's power. She transforms her own dark into her own light. She sees her private shadows - and loves them. She meets her emotional depths - and owns it. She faces her private fears of separation - and rises above the illusion. She takes responsibility for her truth, and where she has repressed herself, and how she has unconsciously dimmed her own light - and she makes a sacred commitment to herself that those lessons are now complete. She dives down deep into herself only to emerge as a more beautiful version of her own energy - refined, commanding, strong, renewed. She is the source of her Self and she is always in a state of greater becoming. She is unlimited potential and unchained possibilities.

In other words, she pretty much rocks the kasbah.

I reference my own spiritual growth journey throughout this book as a case study to clarify and amplify points, but my story is just one example of a Trapeze Artist's experience. As I mentioned earlier, there are unlimited ways in which the journey unfolds. It is never the same known path each time, but there are repetitive themes and stages that show up along the way. Some stages may be longer than others; some parts of the journey may be more intense or personal or monumental. Stages may overlap each other, while other stages may be skipped. The journey is unique to each of us based on what we are here to learn, master, complete, balance, heal at a Soul level.

There are eleven stages of the journey that pertain to today's modern heroine and spiritual growth. Additionally, the journey can be understood through five types of consciousness and two main perspectives, the Elevator and the Spiral. Let's get clear on key definitions and terms before we move through the eleven stages.

CONSCIOUSNESS, SPIRITUALITY, and RELIGION

Consciousness is the understanding that everything around us has meaning associated with it. Everything has consciousness because everything has energy. Becoming more conscious is an opening to greater awareness about the interconnectedness of all things, including all energies beyond the realms of the five senses. Exploring consciousness invites expansion into higher levels of awareness. From the words we say and the actions we take, to our food, numbers, rocks, animals, geographic locations, and everything else around us (a rather large category), all energies hold consciousness.

Consciousness involves many overlapping

factors that contribute to an energetic whole. On an individual level, our emotions, thoughts, vocabulary, and actions all hold a type of consciousness that reflects our personal energy. On a global scale, humanity is collectively creating a level of consciousness about the human experience, the planet, nature, and our responsibility to the earth. Mass consciousness is a reflection of our collective energy.

Which brings us to another important term: energy. How do you describe the "energy" of someone, a certain place, an important life experience, or the vibration of a room? Energy has multiple meanings, and the definition will vary depending on whether you are talking to an engineer and physicist, or a spiritual teacher and psychic. For the purposes of consciousness, energy is an intangible element that describes the vibration, frequency, and consciousness of a person, place, or experience. An interpretation of energy is also connected to an awareness of its consciousness.

One way to connect with the energy of *anything* is to notice how it makes you feel. For example, how would you describe the energy of a candlelit restaurant with soft glowing lights, bottles of Cristal, and a violinist playing in the corner? Perhaps it makes you feel elegant, calm, and decadent, or it could make you feel uncomfortable, anxious, and stressed about your credit card limits. The energy you perceive of the room will be a reflection of your own programming, thoughts, and beliefs, and this combination creates your conscious, or unconscious, awareness.

Another example of energy to consider is a sports stadium bursting at the seams with yelling fans as the clock counts down to the final seconds of the game. How does the energy of this place feel to you? If you are an extrovert, if may feel exciting, stimulating, and uplifting to be with a crowd of people and have all of your senses feel alive. But if you're an introvert or an Empath, the stadium could feel like too much chaos, too crazy, or overwhelming to your senses because you're also picking up everyone's collective energy. Both experiences of energy have value and awareness.

The same can be said for individuals and animals. Every person and living creature has an energy they exude, often unknowingly, and this is connected to their consciousness. Ever been around a dog that is the life of the party, or a friend who is always the talk of the town? (Depending on your social circle, the dog and the friend may be the same thing.) Their individual energy may be felt as being quite big to you, although the consciousness of their energy could vary between wonderful positivity ("He's the happiest guy I know!") or low-vibrational habits ("He is the worst gossip and a total jerk"). Whatever you give attention to in another also reflects *your* energy and consciousness. Energy is a huge topic, and a full discussion is not included in the scope of this book, but more about specific relationship energies will be shared later in the journey.

Consciousness on the planet has shifted greatly as our modern lives led to more indoor living and conveniences. Numerous ancient cultures and societies all over the world relied on the consciousness of nature to guide daily life, including Egyptians, Mayans, Aboriginal Australians, and Polynesians. The sun rising and setting, seasonal changes, watching the cycles of trees and vegetation, paying attention to the habits of animals, documenting the stars, and other essential practices were all referenced as guiding energies of life. There was a greater respect for, and reliance upon, the natural world, and many cultures and people looked to these elements for understanding, direction, and knowledge that contributed to their consciousness. Advanced civilizations still do.

Now we look to Tweets, blog posts, "gurus", politics, and the nightly news, just to name a few areas, for deeper understanding about our lives. Humanity has turned its attention to modern life conveniences, technology, machines, and a different form of living - or survival - that exudes a different type of consciousness. Advanced living does not necessarily equal advances in consciousness. Instead, expanding consciousness is more of a personal choice towards greater self-knowing. As you raise your consciousness, you open up to the awareness that nothing is random or accidental. *Everything happens for a reason* perfectly describes looking at something, anything, from a higher level of consciousness. Interpretations of "a reason" will depend on the type of consciousness you are embodying. More about the five types of consciousness on the planet now will be described in just a few paragraphs.

Essentially, activating greater consciousness in our lives is a connection to higher levels of awareness and energies. There is no single way to do this, hence the beauty of a spiritual growth journey. But what does "spiritual" mean?

I reference the term "spirituality" often throughout this book, and that word has many different definitions to many different people. Here is how I define spirituality, as compared to religion:

Religion requires a communal agreement around values, morals, philosophy, and understanding. Religion involves groups and/or communities of people gathered around shared definitions, usually seeking to sustain, uphold, and perhaps spread their beliefs and values. Religion involves a connection to a supreme entity, often, but not always, through a hierarchical system, and typically includes organizations, initiations, books, and other ancient or modern resources.

Spirituality, on the other hand, is individually-based. It may be as uniquely defined and varied as every person on the planet. A person can define themselves as spiritual with no connection to religion, or a person may define themselves as spiritual *and* be connected to a religious community.

Spirituality and religion can overlap and be contradictory. Religion can be called a spiritual practice, but spirituality is not necessarily a religious practice. Religion is community-based; spirituality can be community-involved or individually-based. A spiritual group may connect over shared religious values, but a spiritual person can have their own non-religious-affiliated values.

And perhaps most notably, spirituality is a bigger umbrella concept that includes ALL religions as channels to connecting with God energy. In this book, spirituality is a personal, individually defined way of connecting with God, Source, the Universe, Spirit, or an all-loving, Divine energy that is within everyone and everything, and is not tied to a religious organization.

With the addition of consciousness, spirituality and religion can vary considerably. There can be great ignorance and righteousness in either one, and there can be immense Love and acceptance in both. Additionally, each type of consciousness offers a way of understanding spirituality, religion, and the world around us. Let's take a look at each type of consciousness that is active on the planet now.

THE FIVE TYPES OF CONSCIOUSNESS

There are currently five dominant types of consciousness present today, co-existing, spreading, retracting. I am specifically identifying these as *types* of consciousness and not *levels* because *levels* implies hierarchy or dominance. Using the word *type* is highly intentional as a way to move beyond the polarities of good and bad; right and wrong; better and worse. Each type of consciousness offers a different perspective, understanding, and opportunities for growth. Each type has value in providing information and describing experiences. Each type also allows us to *choose* what perspective is best for our individual, and collective, growth. The five types of consciousness are:

Separation Consciousness: Everything Happens To Me

Earth Consciousness: What You See Is What You Get

Heart Consciousness: I Am You And You Are Me

Awakening Consciousness: I AM Powerful In All Ways

Cosmic Consciousness: I AM An Eternal Being In An Eternal Universe

SEPARATION CONSCIOUSNESS: EVERYTHING HAPPENS TO ME

Separation Consciousness is based on the illusion of powerlessness. It is believing that your opportunities, your choices, and your circumstances are outside of yourself. Separation Consciousness includes Poverty Consciousness and Victim Consciousness, as well as other terms that support how we may limit ourselves and deny our innate power. This is the most unconscious of all energies, and as such, can create a vicious circle of unconscious life actions including thoughts, words, direction, and emotions that perpetuate feeling like a victim in one's own life.

Separation Consciousness is energized by the Ego-Mind's fears - all of them! Pick a fear, any fear, and you are tapping into the m.o. of unconscious energy that keeps you the furthest from your innate power. Unconscious emotional and mental loops may include blame, rejection, abandonment, shame, guilt, and lack of any kind, including financial, emotional, creative, mental, or energetic. Separation Consciousness is also where we may unconsciously give our power away to something outside of ourselves, from exaggerated importance on money and professional status, to blindly following and trusting politicians, kings, and authorities. We are giving our power to what we perceive as being more powerful than ourselves.

It is fair to say, we all have fears of some kind, and we each meet those fears in our own unique way. And this is why each type of consciousness offers us gifts. With Separation Consciousness, we learn more about ourselves, including our deepest fears, unconscious belief systems, limiting thought patterns, righteous assumptions, and potentials for emotional development and understanding. We see where we are unconsciously creating the experience of separation in some way, and the new choices we can potentially make to find our power within anything.

In *The Art of Trapeze*, I shared a few of my deepest experiences with Separation Consciousness that, believe me, I had trouble typing on the screen at first. My Ego-Mind certainly didn't want me to share any hints of vulnerability, and I struggled with what to put out there. Yet I knew these parts were needed for the story to be authentic. One example of Separation Consciousness is, before boldly moving to Paris, I thought, "Who am I to dream big? Who am I to leave a good-enough job and make this daring move?" I had self-limiting thoughts about what I could with my life. But I answered those silly unconscious beliefs by saying, "Who am I NOT to dream big? Who am I to play it small like the whispers of my heart don't matter?" I shared another example of Separation Consciousness with my brief episode of depression in North Carolina, and interestingly, that story strongly resonated with many readers who have had a similar life experience. I explain that experience more deeply later in this book.

A few ways to move through Separation Consciousness include changing self-limiting and self-sabotaging emotions; identifying deep, ugly, fears; asking questions about assumptions and preprogrammed belief systems; and looking at family or ancestry lines for what has been unconsciously passed down to you. Separation Consciousness also has the greatest amount of potential because it is from this place that you can choose to own and use your power more fully to create new experiences.

EARTH CONSCIOUSNESS: WHAT YOU SEE IS WHAT YOU GET

Earth Consciousness is our default starting point for understanding life because it's based on what is around us. Earth Consciousness is energized by the five senses including looking for proof, validation, data, stimuli, what is visible, and what is verifiable. Earth Consciousness is everything we see, touch, hear, taste, and smell, which is why it is the most dominant energy in our lives. From science and medicine, to nature and social media, Earth Consciousness is the basis for our existence as human beings, including the croissants we eat, the wine we drink, and the high heels we flaunt. It is density, form, all materials and music and perfumes and paddleboards and land masses. Look around your surroundings now and there are probably numerous examples of Earth Consciousness everywhere. And by the way, Earth Consciousness is one of the JOYS of being alive in a physical body!

However, when the energy of Earth

Consciousness becomes out of balance, there is an overemphasis on power, proof, validation, stimuli, and an excessive Ego-Mind drive. This can show up as extreme power through domination and submissive roles; obsession with fame and celebrity; sensationalism, materialism and accumulation of possessions; extreme emotional reactions; competition and war; unconscious judgments; polarity and duality; hierarchy, status, rank, and external authorities. And the list goes on,

Earth Consciousness is also where unconscious karmic energy circulates. Your peer group, colleagues, family, relationships, and acquaintances are often related to unconscious karmic patterns. These karmic energies can include intense emotions, drama, and extreme reactions aimed at proving something, or expressing, or defending, or validating for Ego dominance - the possibilities go on and on. Which is not to say that this is always a bad thing. It's just a matter of understanding what is driving the need. Emotions are often unconscious expressions from the Ego-Mind, and typically have free reign in this energy. More about karmic relationship energies will be discussed later in the journey.

Limitations of Earth Consciousness include esoteric and metaphysical topics, themes, or philosophies that can't be proven or validated. These areas may be extremely confusing to someone operating only in Earth Consciousness. You know, the person who doesn't understand Spirit Guides and the energies of crystals and psychic abilities because there is no proof of how it works. Earth Consciousness is also where the desire to over-prove and compete excessively can lead to false feelings of happiness and success because possessions are used to demonstrate worth. The emphasis is on external rewards and visible satisfaction because that means it's *real.*

But there are great gifts and opportunities with Earth Consciousness, too. Ultimately, we learn what we value in our surroundings, relationships, and daily needs. What job brings you joy? Where do you want to live and spend your days? What food choices are best for you? How do you want to invest your time? What relationships do you want in your life that support, respect, and love you? Essentially, what reality are you creating for yourself on the planet?

In *The Art of Trapeze*, one of my most poignant experiences of Earth Consciousness was when I lived in Portland, Oregon and was trying to figure out what to do with my life. I had an okay job, a decent apartment, two cats, and by all accounts and purposes, a good start after college. Yet I felt compelled to examine my life values, and I started to formulate my More Before list, detailing the experiences I wanted to have in my life based on what could be seen, touched, and created. A process of exploration began that took me out of the status quo and into new possibilities. I claimed a new level of personal power that motivated me to be better and feel in control of my life, which was especially necessary after the Separation Consciousness I experienced in North Carolina.

On that note, the energy of Earth Consciousness may be comforting to Separation Consciousness because it *proves* something you feared: you're not alone, you did a good job, you have value to contribute in your professional life, you can always create a new life for yourself. Earth Consciousness allows us to create goals, experiences, and a lifestyle that matches our individual values.

At this time on the planet, most of the human population operates within Earth Consciousness and Separation Consciousness. But there are more people opening up to Heart Consciousness than ever before.

HEART CONSCIOUSNESS:
I AM YOU AND YOU ARE ME

Heart Consciousness is an energy connected to universal Love-based feelings: Compassion, Forgiveness, Joy, Gratitude, Abundance, and Success. Heart Consciousness is a voice that talks above the noise of the Ego-Mind and guides you to do something that is best for everyone. A feel-good component is active, from donating monthly to the Humane Society, to volunteering two years in the Peace Corps, to choosing to see the best in people even when you're having a rough day.

Heart Consciousness is energized by inclusion, similarities, and connection. We see this energy come alive every time there is a natural disaster of some sort: earthquakes, tsunamis, flooding, and hurricanes offer humanity the opportunity to support each other in times of need. From a spiritual perspective, the higher purpose of these events is to unite people and remind us that we all occupy this blue-and-green marble together. International and domestic travel may open up Heart Consciousness energy as connections with other individuals around the world may remove preconceived notions and stereotypes. Heart Consciousness removes boundaries and labels, and identifies us as brothers and sisters with similar needs of Love, Joy, Forgiveness, and Success.

In *The Art of Trapeze*, I felt the energy of Heart Consciousness strongly as I stood in Room 306 at The Lorraine Motel and tapped into the Love of Martin Luther King, Jr.'s spirit. The experience was unlike anything I had ever felt before and it was a burst of connection to the commonalities our human selves crave. It was my first connection to Heart Consciousness, even though I didn't know at the time that it was pulsing through me.

The expansion of legal rights to historically marginalized populations is an example of increasing Heart Consciousness, with the most recent examples being the right for gay couples to marry in some U.S. states. The increases in charities, non-profit organizations, humanitarian efforts, and volunteer work are prolific examples of Heart Consciousness energies in action. Humans helping other humans; people extending themselves and their energy to be of service in some form, any form. The increase in crowdsourcing initiatives, such as KickStarter, Fundable, and Indiegogo is part of this energy. A professional or volunteer engaged in medicine (doctor, nurse, psychologist, etc.), physical healing, energy work, activism, or any number of service-oriented industries that contribute to the caring of other people may also be demonstrating this energy in a daily manner, depending on the driving intention.

Heart Consciousness is rooted in service, abundance, positivity, and the power of high-vibrational universal feelings. It is the beginning of Self-Help curiosity and New Age topics, including affirmations, positive thought, healing, self-care, and personal growth. Heart Consciousness diminishes the Ego-Mind's drive to dominate and soothes any jagged fears around lack. In one of the last chapters of my memoir, I share observations about the plentitude of nature, the abundance of all necessary elements of our lives, and how we are always supported as we make significant changes in our lives. Heart Consciousness reminds us that there is enough of everything for everyone.

When we consciously choose Heart Consciousness in our lives, we become alive with possibilities, fresh inspirations, and connection. This energy increases even more as we open up to Awakening Consciousness.

AWAKENING CONSCIOUSNESS: I AM POWERFUL IN ALL WAYS

Awakening Consciousness is the understanding that we are each responsible for our own energy, in every situation, all of the time. As a powerful creator of your life, you are the master of your energy, and everything (yep, *everything*) supports your learning and understanding of your energy. Awakening Consciousness is about actively claiming full power over all aspects of your life, from financial and professional experiences, to the karmic lessons, soul work, and belief systems you as a Soul chose to experience in this lifetime.

Awakening Consciousness is understanding the vastness of yourself as a Soul beyond the restrictions of physical, Ego-Mind, or three-dimensional life. You are an eternal being having a temporary experience. As you connect to Awakening Consciousness, the Bigger Picture becomes evident and you open up to more of your innate Soul gifts, talents, and skills, including potential intuition development, psychic abilities, telepathy, channeling, energy work, healing, and other esoteric interests that support you as a Soul.

Awakening Consciousness is energized by

spiritual understanding, authenticity, exploration, meditation, self-reflection, and Soul work. As a result, responsibility, boundaries, discernment, and honoring your authentic path become regular life themes. This is also the "next phase" of New Age topics, including greater wisdom about the purpose of surrender, reincarnation, karmic energies, Soul Agreements, Soul Contracts, Akashic Records, and other areas that support developing your unlimited potential in this lifetime.

With Awakening Consciousness, we learn more about ourselves as beings with eternal Soul energy. We examine our unconscious belief systems, energetic patterns, karmic energies, and how we are powerfully creating everything in our lives. We see each other with a loving, detached lens, knowing that every being is on their own Soul journey and in human form to learn lessons for Soul growth. We detach from the polarity and dualities of Earth Consciousness since every person is viewed as a wise Soul intentionally choosing their experiences. Fear-based emotional reactions and intense feelings are non-existent because every person is honored for what they are choosing, conscious or unconscious, and every person is seen as equally powerful. Respect and acceptance dominates.

A high level of responsibility infuses every choice with this energy. There is an understanding that something doesn't happen to you; it happens *for* your growth and learning. Awakening Consciousness asks, "Why did I create this? What is the best and highest understanding of this experience? And how will I powerfully and intentionally use my energy next?" Combined with Heart Consciousness, this is where mammoth service and gifts to humanity can occur as well as collective evolutions in personal power. Making powerful choices that honor your own energy is a regular guiding intention.

A critical area of life where we can employ Awakening Consciousness is within our relationships. As I described in *The Art of Trapeze*, my relationship with Turhan was a Soul Contract to assist me in trusting myself better. If a relationship stirs deep emotions and learning in your life, it is most likely a pre-chosen lesson by your Soul. More about this vast topic will be examined later as relationships are a huge part of our Awakening journey.

The final type of consciousness on the spiritual growth path connects us to the endless potentials of energy.

COSMIC CONSCIOUSNESS:
I AM AN ETERNAL BEING IN AN
ETERNAL UNIVERSE

Cosmic Consciousness is the understanding that everything is energy and everything is connected to All That Is, including solar systems, stars, planets, and galaxies far, far away. Cosmic Consciousness, also known as God Consciousness and Galactic Consciousness, asks us to look beyond what we know and what we've been taught, to consider that there is much, much more to be discovered about our Universe. We don't know everything; in fact, *we don't know what we don't know.* Are we the only planet with conscious life? Are we the only intelligent beings in the galaxy? Or what if we are the least intelligent beings on the most unconscious planet? What if we're the weakest link, so to speak, and we're collectively rising up to a higher state of awareness? *What if?*

Existing on Earth requires gravity, oxygen, sunlight, and basic survival needs, but what if the time-space continuum is just an illusion and there are more dimensions to experience. What if there are peaceful beings from other planets assisting humanity's evolution on Earth? What if we are not alone in the galaxy and our technology is not as advanced as we assume? What if visitors from other planets are real and happening now? What if aliens are not the bad guys as depicted in Hollywood movies? *What if?*

Cosmic Consciousness is energized by Trust, Peace, Faith, and quantum connections to ourselves as limitless energies existing in multidimensional forms including parallel lifetimes, time travel, advanced technologies, and foreign materials from other planets. It is the awareness of ourselves as part of a bigger energy system that we are only starting to understand And honestly, it could be just enough to confuse our human brains to no end if we try to sort it all out in any type of linear fashion.

With this perspective, we see that we are energetically connected in all ways to all things. We are energy in motion; eternal and spectacular and out of this world. Cosmic Consciousness elevates mundane issues into the ionosphere and raises greater curiosity, including *What's it all about?* There are few concrete human answers at this time, only unending questions. Cosmic Consciousness opens up our understanding of interconnectedness with the desire to continually explore, expand, question, dig in to the new potentials.

In esoteric circles, Cosmic Consciousness is also discussed through connections to the Earth's matrix grid. A matrix grid contains various energy points around the globe, such as ley lines, that connect to powerful universal energies. Ley lines are electromagnetic locations where significant energy emanating from the Earth is strong and influential. Numerous sacred sites are built on ley lines and power centers, including pyramids, shrines, cathedrals, architectural structures, and symbolic relics from ancient cultures. These locations are physical connections to the multiple energies of Cosmic Consciousness on the globe. Many sites on the matrix grid are known for healing, well-being, and activations of greater consciousness because of their rare energies. Ancient cultures were highly connected to Cosmic Consciousness through the cycles of the natural world and their advanced spiritual knowledge that was shared verbally through generations.

Cosmic Consciousness includes all forms of energy. It is a uniting, vast field infused with all potentials and probabilities. There is a recognition that everything is energy, and everything has a contribution to make, including the other four types of consciousness.

As we embark on the modern heroine's journey of spiritual growth, I'll reference these five types of consciousness regularly through various examples. Here is a quick summary of each one again:

Separation Consciousness: Your power is outside of you and life events happen to you.

Earth Consciousness: You rely on all five senses for proof and validation of what is real in life.

Heart Consciousness: You are energetically connected to everyone through the higher energies of Love, Joy, Peace, Forgiveness, and Compassion.

Awakening Consciousness: You are a purposeful Soul who has chosen specific lessons, themes, and areas of growth in this lifetime.

Cosmic Consciousness: You are an endless stream of energy that is connected to everything and the All That Is.

Each of these five types of consciousness is an understanding of energy. Each one offers us experiences to know ourselves better, lessons to learn, and higher perspectives around our power. And present in each consciousness is choice. *Everything is choice.* What you choose to explore is a choice. How you use your energy is a choice. How you interpret events, situations, relationships, thoughts, emotions, and what is best for you is a choice. Employing each type of consciousness is a choice.

However. We don't reside in one type of consciousness continuously or permanently because energy is always in motion. Everything on Earth that endures must grow, change, and flow. Nature is a perfect example of this continual process, especially since nature has survived on the planet longer than anything else. Since our lives, thoughts, feelings, actions, and everything else are always in motion, it's important to understand that every type of consciousness is in flux, too.

Multiple types of consciousness can be active in our lives at the same time. For example, on a calm Tuesday night you may declare, "I love my husband to the moon and back! He is an amazing man doing the best he can for our family every day. I'm so blessed." Then 15 hours later at work, you find yourself muttering, "My boss is the worst man on the planet for making me do this project. What a jerk."

This is a classic example of expressing Heart Consciousness for your husband, who feels your heart with joy, and Separation Consciousness for your boss, whom you perceive as overpowering you and removing your joy. Moving between different types of consciousness, especially within relationships, happens unconsciously depending on numerous factors. Another example of experiencing two types of consciousness in your life is feeling powerful about your spiritual growth (Awakening Consciousness) and then harboring deep self-worth issues around money (Separation Consciousness) and believing you will never have enough.

With so much energy swirling around, let's take a look at how we can consciously choose to move between different types of consciousness with the Elevator or the Spiral.

THE ELEVATOR AND THE SPIRAL

When your boss is a jerk, how do you rise above it? When you feel stuck with money problems, how do you change your perspective? There are two great visuals for moving through these energies: the Elevator, ran by the Ego-Mind, and the Spiral, guided by the Soul. Each method offers a unique perspective and experience. Let's start by looking at the Elevator (since you know the Ego-Mind wants to go first).

The Elevator
The Ego-Mind drives the Elevator. Imagine a

well-dressed concierge operating an immaculate elevator, and observe how he can only direct the car to go up and down. It is simplistic, safe, and easy to understand; plus, a form of control is maintained. The Elevator provides security because it can only go north and south, and therefore, it is easy to interpret events in a straight-forward manner that supports the Ego-Mind's prime functions. Life is good when things go up; life is bad when things go down. It also simpler to live life at the same speed as others, and easy to compare where you are at in relation to others. The Elevator supports staying with a peer group, following the pack, blending in with the crowd, and evaluating life based on hierarchy, accumulation, and status.

The Elevator thrives in Separation Consciousness and Earth Consciousness because it is looking for safety; evaluating what can be gained and lost; and determining how to get ahead for survival. Because the Ego-Mind is primarily concerned with its needs being met, it will create expectations and attachments and goals and resentments. The Ego-Mind is always so, so busy.

For example, the Elevator is not motivated to travel off the known path or push beyond the boundaries. Safety is preferred. Don't rock the boat. Stay in control. Why step outside the comfort zone and explore something foreign or odd or weird? In terms of spiritual growth, the Elevator wants to stay with the masses and be connected to what everyone else is doing. The Ego-Mind thrives within a pack and looks for competitive opportunities to stand out within the group, but it won't go off the Elevator's route. This can also lead to denying authenticity out of fear of the unknown and a perceived loss of control or power.

The Elevator rises and falls between Separation Consciousness, Earth Consciousness, and the penthouse suite, Heart Consciousness. Heart Consciousness is still relatively safe and known to the Ego-Mind, especially as it engages positive feelings and connections with others. But this is also where the Ego-Mind will resist building a connection to the unknown territories of Awakening Consciousness and Cosmic Consciousness. The Elevator wants to stay on the known up-and-down route with everyone else, and rely on what can be validated.

Most people live, exist, and maneuver their lives on the Elevator. Just as Earth Consciousness is our default programming, the Elevator is our standard way of understanding the world around us. Unless "a crisis" of some sort occurs to push one's Ego-Mind beyond the perceived safety of Earth Consciousness and a search for greater understanding. "The crisis" could be a physical accident, financial changes, professional questioning, the end of a significant relationship, or even a crisis of faith. We begin asking deeper questions about life, our purpose, our belief systems, and ultimately, *Who am I in the world*? Usually, something external spurs you forward to seek deeper questions about your existence. It may be interpreted as random, or synchronistic, or completely unexpected. If the Ego-Mind doesn't recognize it as being on the Elevator's path, it could even be deemed as crazy, or weird, or untrue. But from the perspective of Awakening Consciousness, your Soul has actually created the experience of "a crisis" to move you forward into these new levels of growth.

The first chapter of *The Art of Trapeze* involves my inner crisis around professional direction. With nothing to lose, I met with a psychic who opened me up to a broader understanding about my life, my options, and universal energy. A huge shift occurred that took me out of my inner Elevator approach to life where I was unknowingly limiting what I could create, experience, and be. My life perspective expanded immensely when I chose to explore beyond what my Ego-Mind knew. It was a risk to venture into unknown territory where nothing was known, promised, or seen. I had to choose to get off the Elevator to move into new potentials and possibilities.

A pivotal element of spiritual growth is switching from the Ego-Mind's limitations in running the show to a new energetic priority where you are continually connected to your Soul's loving perspective. Imagine standing on top of a building, above the penthouse suite, and looking for a new way to grow. At this point, an essential choice is presented: the decision to leap! If you are up for it, and willing to take a chance to explore beyond what you can see and beyond the known path of the Elevator's route, you can choose to make the leap to the Spiral.

The Spiral

Soul energy guides the Spiral approach to moving through consciousness. The Spiral is a continual movement of energies: fluid and flowing, graceful and continual. Imagine a Spiral in your mind's eye right now. It can be wide and expansive, thin and long, huge or narrow or tall or in the shape of a Christmas tree. There is no beginning and no end. It can collapse into one flat plane, like a plate, or expand out wider than the Earth and cover the globe, then the galaxy, then your friends in other galaxies. The Spiral swirls on to infinity. If you can imagine yourself standing on top of that building still, imagine the Spiral spinning around the outside of the structures. You can look up and not see the end of it, but once you look for it, it appears. The Spiral appears because you chose to see that it exists.

Within the Spiral's energy, there is no good or bad; no right or wrong; no separation or hierarchy or judgment. Every energetic place on the Spiral is valuable because everything is an area of growth, learning, and connection. Lessons are available in all places, and improvements happen all the time, at your own pace, in your own way. Continuity, flow, openness, and acceptance are prominent energies of the Spiral. You are always exactly where you need to be.

Awakening Consciousness and Cosmic Consciousness exist effortlessly on the Spiral because they are energies connected to your Soul's power. Awakening Consciousness is the understanding that you are a powerful being and Cosmic Consciousness is the understanding that you are connected to everything. The Spiral is non-linear and can glide anywhere instantly, moving you away from any fears and actively returning you to a place of inner power.

The Spiral *is* connected to all types of consciousness, but the energy must be invited into the space. You must initiate the request. For example, when you experience a fear around money and temporarily move into Separation Consciousness, you have the option of inviting in a higher perspective around the gifts of these feelings. *What am I learning about how I use money? Where am I perceiving myself as powerless with finances?* These questions open you up to your internal power, and then the Spiral can spin you up to a higher energy source of Love, Peace, Gratitude, Joy, and Abundance. This is where you connect with the wisdom of an experience. Perhaps the answer you hear is: I am temporarily feeling fears around financial lack because *it represents an unconscious self-limiting belief I've carried for years*, or *I was not shown it was safe to be financially powerful*, or *I am afraid of having money and always losing it*, or (*your answer here*).

Let's briefly compare this perspective to the Elevator's perspective that it is more desirable to move up and maintain a secure perch. The Elevator approach to this issue would be that you need to get more money and the problem will be fixed. Go UP, get a raise, and things get better! Yet status and security isn't necessary on the Spiral because from the Soul's perspective, you are *always* safe and important and connected. Your financial status is just a reflection of energy and you can always change the energy. There is value in every experience of energy. The Ego-Mind does not have the perspective of infinity, or continual connection, or unlimited potentials because it is always searching for proof, validation, security.

Since the Spiral is connected to Spirit and your Soul, its energy is very high-vibrational and will only connect you with empowering questions about all experiences: *What am I learning? What is the highest possible understanding of this relationship, emotion, or situation? How can I be more powerful in this experience now?* When you ask the bigger questions that include your power, you connect to the greater gifts of healing, lessons, and growth. The Spiral's perspective will open you up to more than Separation Consciousness, Earth Consciousness, or Heart Consciousness because it is energetically above any human perspective. The Spiral honors both your choices as a Soul and how you use energy as a person, and will not try to force your energy to do something. That is soooo the Ego-Mind's tactic.

The energy of the Spiral came through strongly in *The Art of Trapeze* during my conversation with God. How often do we judge ourselves, or feel guilty, or miss the bigger meaning because we thought we did something wrong? The Spiral will open you up to a higher level of consciousness that says, *You can't get anything wrong. You can only get it right.* This message might not satisfy the ambitious, specific Ego-Mind, but it does offer a new channel to Self-Love and the endless potentials of energies.

I also want to be clear that both the Elevator and the Spiral offer gifts. The Elevator has a beneficial purpose in our complicated world where multiple energies regularly exist. It can be easier and highly valuable to navigate life more simply on the Elevator in order to move between Good or Bad; Yes or No; Right or Wrong. In fact, since we are surrounded by stimuli from all directions, we *need* ways to evaluate what is Good or Bad, Right or Wrong, Yes or No. It would be too exhausting to always determine the highest possible answer to every little thing all the time. The Elevator is simplistic, and can be very useful in guiding us through everyday conversations, key details, and prioritizing those never-ending to-do lists.

In terms of your Soul's growth, the Spiral shows where we are learning, healing, growing, and owning more of our true power. Another gift of the Spiral is that it reveals unconscious patterns, thoughts, feelings, and belief systems in one area of life so you can see if that energy is active in all areas of your life. You don't have two brains (unless cloning has really taken off since the publication of this book). You have a filter in which you perceive the world, your place in it, your identity, your power. How you interpret one story is how you interpret every story. How you perceive one event is how you perceive all events. How you view yourself financially could be how you also view yourself spiritually. The Spiral will highlight filters such as unconscious beliefs, thoughts, and mental programming loops that have never been questioned, examined, or challenged.

The willingness to *open up* to a higher perspective is part of the leap from the Elevator to the Spiral. Call it a leap of faith, a leap of trust, a leap of consciousness; it all comes down to making the choice to venture further into your spiritual growth and energetic power. Are you willing to view an experience, relationship, situation, anything above the limitations of the Ego-Mind's simplicity and transition to a higher perspective? For example, the Ego-Mind may declare a job termination as a failure and a loss, but from a Soul perspective, the career transition is a huge success because the lessons, healing, and growth from that position are now complete. The Spiral's energy will always enhance your personal power and connect you to a loving perspective with a higher consciousness.

Ideally, the Ego-Mind and Spirit work together concurrently to guide you to higher levels of spiritual growth and personal actualization. Remember the visualization you just did about how the Spiral looks in your mind's eye? Now visualize that same Spiral energy circling up, up, up while the Elevator keeps pace in the middle. Ahhh, feel the flow, harmony, and alignment. Intentionally connecting the best of both energies creates an energetic win-win. After all, we have Ego-Mind energy for a reason; it's not something we need to completely ignore and throw away.

The Ego-Mind tends to get a bad rap because it is an overused energy on the planet that is taken to extremes many ways, many times. Instead of trying to get rid of it, the Ego-Mind just needs another assignment. It wants to support you, and champion you, and get things done, and cheer you on to be the best you can be. At it's highest expression, the Ego-Mind is what gets you out of bed each day with the goal of making the most of everything that comes your way. The Ego-Mind has determination, inspiration, focus, and pride. It drives us towards our goals and gives us courage in meetings to speak up, or to complete a marathon, or to try something new, or to make each day productive. It can be a healthy support system when the energy is in cooperation with your highest intentions, an ability to Trust, and feeling confident in your actions. You become an unstoppable force of awesomeness. This is a wonderful place to own your power, believe in your dreams, and know you are at the best possible place on your path right now. The Ego-Mind is not the enemy. It just needs to be re-trained to support your Soul's growth without trying to run the show all the time. (And you know the Ego-Mind is the one who wanted the lightsaber in the first place.)

The Spiral and the Elevator working in harmony is the essence of being a spiritual human. Trusting your Soul's energy and honoring your human needs harnesses an energetic combination like nothing else. This is where a Trapeze Artist becomes an unstoppable force at following her heart and believing in the vastness of her dreams. She moves from the unconscious limitations of her Ego-Mind into the essence of her conscious power, the heart of herself, and expands from that space to believe that everything is always happening for her best and highest good.

So now we're going to take all of these concepts into the spiritual growth journey. We've covered the influential importance of Joseph Campbell's the hero's journey; the unlimited definitions of a Trapeze Artist; defined consciousness, spirituality, and religion; reviewed the five types of consciousness on the planet; and summarized the energetic offerings of the Elevator and the Spiral. It's time to venture forward into the eleven stages of spiritual growth and witness how a modern heroine's journey of consciousness uses all of these elements as she claims more of her personal mastery.

Let the higher levels of Trust begin.

1.
THE UNCONSCIOUS WORLD

AND IT WAS ANOTHER dry Thursday of some month of some year in her life. Her pulse was beating mildly. She knew how to live between cups of coffee and glasses of wine, morning news and evening sitcoms, soft slippers and stiff high heels and back to soft slippers again. The daily routine was known. The life to-do list was stocked full.

Yet a discomfort grew.

An inner tension rises and falls more often, more regularly, signaling to her that *there must be something more than this.* Something. Anything? *PLEASE.* An adventure, an idea, an inspiration. Or even just a good glimpse of herself in the mirror where her mouth whispers back a jolting insight. She is unknowingly naive and innocent about her full potential because she doesn't know what it could even be. *Is there more about my energy, my life choices, my spiritual connections to understand?* She may look to her mother, sisters, best friends, colleagues, or boss for clues to her potential and possibilities, but she still feels unsatisfied. Stuck. Frustrated. Cluttered and unclear.

Little does she know, this is a beautifully delicious place to be. A Trapeze Artist is warming up to her own inner energy. She is being nudged forward by unseen forces and indescribable sensations that taunt her to *just try* what is coming up to her awareness. Little does she know, the discomfort is actually supporting her, although it may not feel that way. Little does she know, the internal tension is a gift towards greater action although it might appear to be the opposite.

She is a common citizen in the Unconscious World and yet has no idea that there is any other place to be. This is all she knows. *She doesn't know what she doesn't know.* And yet her energy is slowly, gradually, expanding beyond the confines of the Unconscious World that has held her comfortable for years. It has guaranteed a certain path, a known way towards success and happiness and a life well lived. Nothing to complain about, really.

The Unconscious World is the landscape of Earth Consciousness and Separation Consciousness that is everywhere. It is all she sees because it is all she has known. A Trapeze Artist is an unconscious participant in Earth Consciousness, and occasionally dabbles in Separation Consciousness when she finds herself believing her happiness and true power are in the next job title, the bigger dwelling, the newer car. She has done what she was supposed to do to find happiness: graduated from college, secured a paycheck, upgraded her grocery store selections to organic, volunteered regularly and often in her community. She enjoys the comforts of this life and feels grateful for her achievements. This is what she knows and has followed; nothing else has been modeled or demonstrated for her. She lives in the sanctuary and relative simplicity of Earth Consciousness. And it's good. There is much to be grateful for.

Except something keeps pulling at her heart. Maybe this isn't the only experience for her. Maybe there is more. Maybe there is something beyond this. Maybe? She silently questions her spiritual understandings and wonders what other knowledge is out there for her to explore.

Back to the dry Thursday of some month where her inner desire to follow a dream grows. It is becoming too strong to be ignored for one more trip around the clock. A Trapeze Artist finally understands, and sees, and feels in her heart of hearts that she really does want more than *this*. She might not be able to specifically identify what 'more' is, exactly, but she knows on some level it is more of herself. More of her private dreams, a bigger vision. More of her life. A quiet calling continues, the whispers growing louder and louder.

She nestles into her soft slippers and considers what the whispers could mean. Could she really have a bigger dream to follow? Could she really move beyond what she has now and follow the nudges, the push? Could it be safe to leave the comforts of this platform and jump to another? Could she trust what she doesn't know?

She sinks back into the Unconscious World and looks around. It begins to feel too small.

2.
THE CALL OF HER SOUL

WHETHER IT'S A DREAM, a discomfort, an impatience, or an unconscious desire, *something* internal moves a Trapeze Artist forward. She knows it's time to make a change. She feels it on an energetic level that she can't quite describe and maybe doesn't even want to put into words. How does one adequately share their own knowingness, their own truth? It is a personal and sacred language, an inner message between her and her Soul. The feeling is too strong for the constriction of sounds.

She may not feel completely ready, or absolutely certain, or totally convinced about what to do and how to do it perfectly. But she knows it is time. She has to go for it. She is ready to trust the feelings as messages of faith. It is time to answer the Call of her Soul.

She jumps.

She leaves one platform of her life in the Unconscious World, with its known routines, and secure parking spots, and favorite television shows, and ventures off into the new world of What's Unknown. She has uncertainties, but also undercurrents of excitement. She has slight anxiety, but also ripples of quiet exhilaration. She has questions, but also huge, mammoth doses of trust. She knows she ultimately carries everything she needs for the journey ahead because the timing is right. It's now.

When she finally answers the Call of her Soul, a permanent shift occurs in a Trapeze Artist's energy. She moves away from the inner tension and silent conflicts. She has made a choice about where to direct her energy, and upon making this commitment, numerous unseen forces rise up to meet her in this place. She is answering a question she has postponed, and it now leads her to a new inner experience of uplifting feelings. Peace. Delight. Potentials. Joy. These are the energies she has been looking for in her daily life but wasn't able to connect with because nothing else could match the vibration of her Soul's energy.

It was up to her to make the choice to connect with her Soul's message, nudges, whispers.

And in the moment when she said YES - quietly, softly, with eyes closing in sweet surrender - she was saying YES to her heart, her truth, her deepest desires. She was saying YES to this part of herself for the first time.

In hindsight, a Trapeze Artist will realize that the inner tension she felt right up until she said YES was the quaking of her Heart Consciousness rumbling and tumbling inside her tectonic plates. Her Soul was shaking up her inner energy source to encourage her to *go for it* and leave the restrictions of what she could see, prove, touch behind. *Follow the dreams you are here to experience. Listen to the whispers that are so easy to tune out for too long. Trust that there is a bigger version of You to explore.*

She could easily stay in the Unconscious World she has always known, and her Soul would honor her free will to do so. On the Spiral, her Soul's growth is always right on time no matter what decision she makes. There is no deadline, although her Elevator perspective might say she should have done this ten years ago, or last month, or before now. Her Soul supports any path, any dream, any timing that is right for her. So why not go for the biggest possible one now?

It is the defining moment where she leaps ahead, following the Call of her Soul, to explore new levels of spiritual understanding.

Until she freaks out about her choice.

3.
REFUSING HER SOUL'S WHISPERS

HER BEAUTIFUL EGO-MIND WILL provide numerous reasons not to do something. These could be reasons she's believed before, or excuses she used her whole life, or temporary fears that arise out of unconscious mental patterns about limiting herself. Or staying small. Or not being ready. Or waiting for *that other thing* to happen first. But when she returns to that quiet moment when she powerfully and deliberately said YES, she will feel the energy of the decision push her forward as she leaps.

Once a Trapeze Artist has landed in her new experience, and gets her temporary grounding, and feels empowered with her decision, she will come up against her first fear of failure. Those Ego-Mind messages will pop up louder when things don't happen, stop signs appear, and extreme doubts blare more loudly. She will wonder why she left the

Unconscious World in the first place.

Embarking on a journey of spiritual understanding initially brings up many questions, foreign concepts, and an overwhelming array of potential tangents. The territory is odd and uncomfortable, and she all of a sudden feels very alone. She may envy those living in Earth Consciousness because they are safe, secure, reliable. She will also appreciate it more and realize that maybe fitting in with everyone else and having a regular routine wasn't so bad. A Trapeze Artist will feel the pull to return to her former life, her known desk, the Thursday night television line-up. It's all waiting for her right there if she pulls a quick U-turn.

Why not go back?

Maybe this big risk isn't worth it. Maybe it's not meant to be. Maybe she isn't supposed to find an apartment in Paris or make a life here. Maybe the timing is off. Maybe she was foolish, or disillusioned, or silly. Or wrong. She is looking in the mirror, face to face with her inner fears. The deeper fear says: *What if she can't make this happen?*

Breathe.

In this phase, little does she know, she is not alone. A higher supportive energy is just around the corner, waiting to meet her in this hour of need.

When she honestly and bravely identifies her ultimate fear of rejection, of abandonment, of judgment, of failure, she then releases that energy from within her being and moves it through her consciousness. She looks at the fear of failure and declares she is stronger than that voice. She identifies any self-sabotaging actions she unconsciously resorts to, and insists on doing something differently starting now.

At this stage, a Trapeze Artist is given the choice to turn back, or continue on. Will she make a new choice in how she lives her life or continue to make the same choices she always has? This is the first threshold of personal commitment to herself. It's not about the stop signs, or the delays, or what is not happening that she was counting on. It's about choosing herself and her spiritual growth regardless of external *anything*.

She can always turn back, or delay, or give herself a list of excuses. In fact, there are a million reasons *not* to do something. But there is only way to do it. And that's to do it. So she chooses to do it.

4.
OPENING UP TO A GREATER POWER

A TRAPEZE ARTIST HAS leaped forward with gusto, and unexpectedly hit a brick wall. She may feel that all is lost, or she messed up, or she made a terrible choice and this isn't going to work. Yet she chose to stick with the Call of her Soul and consciously decided to Trust and believe in the power of her dreams. She just needs a bit more support, a mentor, a guide, a solution to these limitations right now.

In the Unconscious World, she might not have known a bigger energy was available because she didn't have to rely on it regularly. She could navigate life based on the joys of Earth Consciousness - everything important was on television, in a magazine, in her bank account, in an email. She could go about her day without requiring something bigger to rely on as long as the internet was working.

But out here, in the unknown territory of answering the call of her Soul, a Trapeze Artist finds herself needing more support than she has ever known before. The brick wall a Trapeze Artist experiences is a reflection of her own internal energy that is afraid. When she calls the fear out for what it really is - no more smoke and mirrors or sailing down the river of denial - then she can also call in something bigger and safer to take her forward. This is the first connection to the Spiral energy. Call it God, Source, Spirit, or the Universe, whatever feels right. As she crossed the first threshold and made a commitment to herself, she feels this energy around her in ways she didn't notice before. She is exactly where she needs to be at all times and she has everything she needs within. She *chooses* to realize she is safe on this journey.

A Trapeze Artist then strengthens her resolve in herself, in her choice, and in her ability to succeed. She trusts in herself as an energy bound with Spirit. It's a brief glimpse into her deepest power as she fully owns herself and all of her energy. She's in it now *for reals*. She's here, with all of her heart, to make a dream happen. She regroups, re-focuses, and makes a certain choice during this uncertain time. Her commitment to herself is cemented. This new inner strength infuses all of her actions.

She rises above the limitations of what can be seen or proven, as Earth Consciousness would point out, and instead acknowledges herself as a creator of the energy she seeks. She is now living with a higher level of trust in herself, where Heart Consciousness and Awakening Consciousness thrive. She is on the Spiral, confirming that she is always in charge of her life, her emotions, her intentions.

And just like that, after elevating the energy with trust, a solution arrives. Money comes through, a new partner arrives, a Divine development happens, or she finds a charming apartment in Paris, mere blocks south of the Eiffel Tower.

An encouraging effect of operating with higher levels of trust is that it is completely internal. No one else can do it for her, and no one else can take it away from her. Like meditating. She had to trust what she couldn't see, remain strong in her energetic intentions, and take actions to support the desired outcome. There is no visual, linear chart depicting, "This Is How You (and everyone else) Trusts." It is experiential, and only known through doing. When a Trapeze Artist is in full control of her energy, she can fire herself up with bursts of trust, growing self-love, and uncompromising faith in herself. She will have ongoing opportunities to strengthen her self-trust as new situations present themselves on the journey ahead.

After opening up to a greater power, a Trapeze Artist will experience more simple daily delights as she regularly tunes into her intuition, like finding the perfect winter coat because she followed her inner guidance to turn left down a new street. Or she will act with confidence in moments that require split-second decisions, such as disembarking an international flight five minutes before departure because her cats cannot travel on the plane.

At this stage in the journey, a Trapeze Artist has committed to answering the Call of her Soul, has overcome a few inner fears, opened up to a higher power as her co-pilot, and resolved to trust herself even more. From this space, her ability to manifest exactly what she desires takes off. She starts to meet new friends, old energies, and handsome lovers from past lives long ago.

5.
MANIFESTING, SOUL CONTRACTS, PAST LIVES, OH MY!

Significant and unexpected developments are now brewing for a Trapeze Artist. She is pushed to go bigger in her life, challenged to be more of herself, and encouraged to stretch a little farther into her own energy. She is opening, deepening, trusting her path like never before, and it feels exhilarating and terrifying, essential and optional. Connecting with her burgeoning internal power becomes more natural. She has experienced miracles overnight and knows she can rely on her gut-level intuition for guidance at all times. And it is from this place that she manifests relationships, tests, and opportunities in the form of Soul Contracts, past life connections, and incomplete energies as new areas in her spiritual growth.

Let's step back from the journey for a moment and look at more spiritual concepts to understand why a Trapeze Artist will connect with certain people, allies, and manifestations at this stage.

Manifesting is the magnetic pull of like energies coming together, and this magnetic attraction occurs within every type of consciousness. We've come to associate "manifesting" with the glamour and excitement of a great new opportunity, money pouring in, a fabulous new relationship, and unexpected, miraculous developments. And these certainly *are* examples of creating something desirable in one's life. However, manifesting and the oh-so-popular Law of Attraction phenomenon doesn't all of a sudden "start working" once you hear about the concept, buy a book, take a class, or focus on spiritual pursuits. You are *always* magnetically attracting expressions of energy, all the time, every minute of every day, based on your energy. Owning cars that always break down, repetitive relationship patterns, unfulfilling job choices, lack of financial flow, and being miserable are *also* examples of manifesting, albeit within a different type of consciousness, which is to say, within a different field of energy. A Trapeze Artist is at the stage where she is attracting exactly what she needs to learn now based on her energy.

And here's the kicker: *Energy doesn't care what you want.* Think about that for minute. Energy doesn't care what you request, do, intend, desire, or pray for every night on bended knees. You can intend for anything - *anything* - from a piece of strawberry gum, to a six-pack of craft beer, to an amazing job advancement, to a new group of friends, to a dream vacation with a rich Latin lover who only has eyes for you, except when he needs his eyes to prepare a gourmet five-course meal to demonstrate how much he cherishes you on a Tuesday night. Energy doesn't judge, or alter, or stop and think about your request. Energy just does its thing based on you, like a magnet that is always on, or a neutral courier who constantly brings in what you are signaling out. Every person is the master of their own energy. Yet it is often unconscious energy that governs our lives until we start to see how powerful we are and how we can choose to direct our energy consciously.

The manifesting formula is specialized for each person based on their soul lessons, karmic energies, past lives, soul contracts, life experiences, and of course, the almighty wild card, free will. Initially, it is a complex formula that each person has the *choice* to explore - or not! - and discover more about for themselves. No one says you have to do spiritual work. No one says you must figure this stuff out, or ELSE. No one is requiring everyone on the planet to be interested in this information. No one is requiring you to dive in and know your own energy on a deeper level and get to the heart of unconscious patterns and make fundamental life changes. No one is making you, right? As you read these words, are your feet being held to the fire? (If you answered yes, probably best to put this book down right about now.)

Nope, there is no requirement to do anything about your energy. Yet on some level, you are making a *choice* to investigate it a bit deeper based on a Call of your Soul for spiritual growth. And there are rewards with this journey because you are choosing to tap into the higher energies of consciousness that are available to you now. As such, you'll notice how manifesting at higher levels of consciousness can be out-of-this-world remarkable, bring incredible joy, open up to more experiences of success, and the list of rewards goes on.

Soul Contracts are one key manifestation because they have the potential to bring unconscious relationship themes to conscious awareness. Soul Contracts, like Soul Agreements, Soul Mates, and Karmic Relationships, are incomplete energies between Souls. They are highly unconscious energies that pervade and circulate in relationships, partnerships, friendships, professional contacts, and especially between family members. (If you've ever felt like *your* family is the most dysfunctional, or craziest, or most dramatic clan on the block, then these relationship definitions may be enlightening. As they say, if you ever need to determine how spiritually evolved you are, just spend a weekend with your family.)

The following insights around Soul Contracts, Soul Agreements, Soul Mates, Soul Groups, and Karmic Relationships explain the energetic differences and similarities that each of us at a Soul level chooses to experience for growth, healing, and greater personal power.

SOUL CONTRACTS

A binding contractual energy, made at a Soul level, to ensure your Soul's growth in this lifetime. The contract is often around an integral life theme (such as owning your power, trusting Self, recognizing Self-worth, etc.) and the theme probably starts with early childhood experiences. Parents can be connected to this theme, as can other family members, childhood friends, and pivotal life events.

In order to grow through the Soul Contract lesson, you need someone (or multiple people) to be "the other" in the scenario. If your dominant lesson is greater Self-trust, someone needs to point out the theme by betraying you. If your lesson is Self-worth, you need opportunities to stand on your own and believe in yourself. If you are here to be more powerful, you may have many experiences of feeling powerless and being disrespected in order to build a stronger core of inner strength. All of these themes, and more, can concurrently exist and overlap in a lifetime; the potential combinations are limitless. A Soul Contract is meant to empower you, but it may bring you to your knees first and be the source of extreme emotional reactions, deep fears, and life-defining experiences. Soul Contracts often have a lot of emotional energy around them, and those feelings are meant to propel you forward because they will probably become too uncomfortable to bear. Quite a brilliant catalyst.

Many people have similar Soul Contract themes in this lifetime around Self-Love and Self-Trust, which is why betrayal, power struggles, disrespect, and other related situations are so prominent on earth at this time. It is also why spiritual awakenings are so significant on the planet because people have had *enough* of the circular themes and are willing to ask deeper, self-probing questions which lead to Awakening Consciousness.

A Soul Contract includes other Souls, but it is also a commitment you made to yourself in this lifetime. After being identified, Soul Contract themes continue and will reappear throughout a lifetime, but you begin to recognize the theme sooner (say, within ten minutes instead of ten years), and then you can consciously make different choices around your actions. This allows you to move through the experience faster (say, in one week instead of twenty years), and you can experience greater detachment, grace, and peace because you know *what it's really about*. For example, if your main Soul Contract is Self-trust and you find yourself betrayed by another person because you didn't trust yourself *yet again*, you will probably move through the emotional reactions and understanding faster because you understand the theme and your responsibility in this situation. Ideally, you arrive at Self-Forgiveness faster than in previous scenarios and with hindsight, know what to do next time to change your experience.

SOUL AGREEMENTS

A Soul Agreement is an area of growth where your Soul is choosing to improve, but it is energetically less formal and less binding than a Soul Contract. A Soul Contract is like being married to a theme whereas a Soul Agreement is dating it. There might be less emotional intensity around the lesson, but somewhere in your awareness, you probably notice that a pattern keeps coming up that can be changed.

For example, you may regularly find yourself in situations with people who see you as a scapegoat of some kind, or as the weakest link, and you never stand up for yourself. Or you may try to get by in multiple situations by contributing as little as possible (financially, emotionally, physically, mentally) because you carry an unconscious energy of entitlement. As a Soul Agreement, you can choose to address the theme head-on, or choose to let it go, or ignore it, or deny it, or go to a party and leave it sitting in the backseat. Yet the energy will routinely show up in various experiences as a window of opportunity for growth, and it will reappear in future lifetimes (oh yes, *it will*).

Soul Agreements may be easier to continually walk away from, but as with all experiences, they are meant to enhance your personal power. What would a completely powerful person with nothing to lose choose to do with their Soul Agreement themes? Like Soul Contracts, Soul Agreements can include other people, but it is essentially an agreement you made with your Soul to change an unconscious energy (habit, pattern, fear) into a higher vibrating expression. Also like Soul Contracts, Soul Agreements continue throughout this lifetime and once mastered, you will move through the energy faster and more powerfully. Instead of leaving it in the back seat, you'll invite it into the party.

SOUL MATE

Any person who helps your Soul to grow is a Soul Mate, but this is not always the romanticized, idyllic version of Soul Mates that pervades pop culture terminology. A Soul Mate can be the most difficult person in your life, a childhood bully, every person you've dated and hated, a crazy work colleague, and/or your best friend. A Soul Mate can also be the high school sweetheart who supports you unconditionally, and chances are their Soul Contract with you is to give you the experience of unconditional love in this lifetime. They are often included in Soul Contracts, Soul Agreements, or other Karmic Relationships.

Soul Mates exist within all types of consciousness and within all areas of life, such as the kind banker you interact with each week who wants you to invest your money wisely, to the crazy lady at work that requires you to be more patient and compassionate on a daily basis, even though you'd rather spill your soup on her lap. Love 'em or hate 'em, all Soul Mates assist your growth in some manner.

KARMIC RELATIONSHIPS

People you have incomplete energetic experiences with from past lives. The energy between you needs to be balanced in order to end circular patterns, emotional reactions, Ego-Mind power roles, and all unconscious habits that thrive in Separation Consciousness and Earth Consciousness.

Many Karmic Relationships appear through jobs and career choices because the professional world is a huge playground that allows numerous energies to co-exist simultaneously, from massive betrayal and power struggles, to trustworthy handshakes and unlimited abundance. When Karmic Relationship energies are balanced (either within yourself or between the parties), or the lesson is learned, or the wound is healed, the professional roles may end or drastically change. The student becomes the teacher, the intern becomes the CEO, the enemies become equal partners.

In family dynamics, these changes can show up as divorce, estrangement, death, separation, reunions, or turning over a new leaf within the relationship. The possibilities and outcomes are based on many factors, including what the karma is, soul lessons, timing, and each individual's free will.

Heart Consciousness is needed in all Karmic Relationships to raise the energy with Forgiveness, Peace, and Gratitude for the lesson. Detachment, self-respect, and acceptance are also required to begin new cycles of growth. Awakening Consciousness reveals the bigger story between the Souls, such as past life scenarios, Akashic Records history, unconscious emotional reactions, and why the Soul chose this experience.

Karmic Relationships always involve other people, but once the past life energy is balanced and the lesson is learned, the relationship connection is over. Resignation letters are sent, a new job opportunity is presented, a divorce is final, or a flight attendant exits down the airplane's emergency slide with a beer in hand. Karmic Relationships can include Soul Mates, and your experiences with them can connected to a Soul Contract and/or a Soul Agreement.

SOUL GROUPS

Clusters of people you've had many lifetimes with for the purpose of mutual growth and support. This almost always includes your immediate family and/or parents who require you to learn something significant for Soul growth, mastery, and personal power. You may meet multiple Soul Groups from various past life scenarios throughout your life, or you may have one significant Soul Group that you stay connected with from birth to death.

There is usually a dominant theme within the group, and there can be complex overlaps in Soul Contracts, Soul Agreements, and Karmic Relationships. Examples of Soul Groups may include childhood friends; co-workers and colleagues; classmates; social circles; immediate and extended families; spiritual groups; sports teams; political allies and rivals; and/or any collection of individuals connected by strong emotions, Ego-Mind energies, and/or mutual growing experiences.

Soul Groups incarnate together to learn, grow, and heal, and to do this, they typically reenact the same themes throughout different lifetimes by changing roles (such as rotating parent/child roles; murderer/victim; political rivals and combat enemies; master/slave; best friends and support systems; plus countless other combinations). Soul

Groups are "working something out" together, often like a tangled knot of energy.

Another example is how everyone in a Soul Group may contribute to an overarching message to benefit others. For example, some Soul Groups choose to die together in horrific circumstances to open humanity up to Love, Forgiveness, and Peace. Souls volunteer for these roles and offer their energy for the good of Heart Consciousness and Awakening Consciousness. Other Soul Groups choose to expand society's definition of Love by challenging norms, protesting laws, and requiring legal changes, such as civil rights, women's rights, and gay rights campaigns. Another Soul Group may live in a small remote community and agree to learn lessons together that they couldn't, or didn't, complete in previous lifetimes.

You can be connected to multiple Soul Groups based on multiple lifetimes of experiences. The combinations are unlimited. Ultimately, Soul Groups remind us we're all connected to each other.

[Please know this is a huge topic that includes more insights than these brief paragraphs cover. I recommend Robert Schwartz's books for greater exploration and understanding: *Your Soul's Plan: Discovering the Real Meaning Of The Life You Planned Before You Were Born* and *Your Soul's Gift: The Healing Power of The Life You Planned Before You Were Born*. I also recommend two books by Dr. Michael Newton, *Journey of Souls: Case Studies of Life Between*

Lives and *Destiny of Souls: New Case Studies of Life Between Lives.*]

After reviewing these five categories, it is important to point out that theses understandings around spiritual relationship energies only exist within Awakening Consciousness. Why is that? A quick review:

Separation Consciousness is disconnected from the Soul's power to choose experiences and has the perspective that unsatisfying relationships, repetitive experiences, settling for what they have, and being stuck in an unfulfilling marriage happens *to* them.

Earth Consciousness wants proof of these relationship dynamics, and the Ego-Mind refuses to see its own responsibility in creating these growing experiences. These terms (Soul Contracts, Soul Agreements, Soul Groups, etc.) probably sound like spiritual jargon because there is no proof to validate them.

Heart Consciousness offers Love-based understanding to these relationship connections, but may idealize situations without fully understanding one's individual power within them. Heart Consciousness may overlook how each person is powerful, and therefore, not see responsibility for their own choices and Soul growth.

Awakening Consciousness is the perspective

that *of course* you as a powerful Soul chose these themes and lessons.

Back to our modern heroine. At this stage of the journey, a Trapeze Artist has most likely encountered a few people connected to her Soul Contracts, Soul Agreements, and Karmic Relationships. In *The Art of Trapeze*, I met both Turhan and Trisha during this phase. Turhan was a wonderful romantic partner because in addition to all of the experiences we had together, I was also learning more about myself in the partnership dynamic.

When connected with the Spiral, we are always learning exactly what we need at the right time. The Ego-Mind might want to deny, or overpower, or minimize a relationship to maintain a form of control, but we always manifest exactly what we need, right when it is needed. Relationships are this reflection. And the same could be said for my new friendship with Trisha. Trisha and I enrolled in the same Master's program at the same small school on the same day in the same European city. Energetically, we showed up for each other at a time when both of us were open and ready for a quality friendship. This connection provided both of us with support, laughter, and an important ally as we followed our individual Calls of the Soul.

Less desirable characters arrive at this stage in her spiritual growth, too. A Trapeze Artist will meet individuals who are not trustworthy, nor good friends, nor supportive allies, nor welcomed acquaintances. She will need to continually rely on her intuition, keen observation skills, and common sense smarts to navigate all relationships, and wisely discern whom to allow on her journey. Some of these individuals may gift her with seeing a Soul Agreement she is ready to address, or support her ability to say 'no' to manipulative trickster energies. Other people may offer her opportunities to disengage from energies she no longer wants to participate in, such as gossip or mean girl antics. From the perspective of Awakening Consciousness, she can understand how other Souls are crossing her path to support her choices and how she always has the power to direct her energy. A Trapeze Artist may also meet these people because they have a past life connection together at this location.

Every place on earth holds an energetic vibration. A Trapeze Artist is energetically drawn to locales where she has incomplete energies from past lives. This is often an unconscious connection, but it's also why the Call of her Soul is so profound. She is guided to necessary locations (coffee shops, neighborhoods, cities, states, countries) to connect with the experiences, relationships, and emotions that her Soul is now ready to complete.

Throughout *The Art of Trapeze*, I reference the multiple places I have lived (Seattle, Washington; Monterey, California; Greenville, North Carolina; Portland, Oregon; Paris, France) and the energetic experiences each locale held for me. I was drawn to each place very clearly at certain times in my life to focus on specific lessons, healings, and areas of growth. For example, I recall always knowing I had to go to school in North Carolina. In hindsight, I saw how this was because I was ready on a Soul level to move the energies of Separation Consciousness through me. In Portland, Oregon, I was ready to open up to a life experience beyond what I had known through Earth Consciousness. In Paris, I created a life-changing experience to open me up more fully to Awakening Consciousness. The energies for another person at these exact same places could be the complete opposite of what I experienced because it is highly personal and specialized; it is uniquely her path.

Additionally, the Call of my Soul was nudging me towards unfinished professional energies in Paris that I was ready to experience. I received not one, but two, highly sought-after offers to work at U.S. Embassies. Getting these two simultaneous placements is highly rare, and it would make me uncomfortable to "toot my own horn" if it wasn't for the understanding that I have strong past life energies in European politics, royalty, and leadership. (For the record, many of us have had past life roles in royalty because our Soul wants to experience the full spectrum of human possibilities, from poverty to prosperity, from extreme power to complete lack of ego. Which explains why we all look so great in tiaras.)

I manifested the amazing opportunity to work for a U.S. Ambassador because my energy was at a place to connect with the energy of that experience. If I had doubted, or resisted, or denied, or self-sabotaged in some way, the connection never would have happened based on my unconscious energies. Instead, I trusted the path as it was shown to me, followed my instincts, and believed in myself. I chose to believe I was worthy of this amazing opportunity, and that level of self-empowerment carried me forward. I had an uncompromising desire to push myself towards the biggest dream and the grandest possible outcome. My Soul's guidance was in charge and I was choosing to trust it with energy on the Spiral and my high heels on the ground (and usually a croissant in hand).

Another example of manifesting a past life connection was when I found an idyllic apartment in a charming village just a few miles from the Versailles Palace. I had no idea this town on the outskirts of Paris even existed until I was guided to it, and then it felt instantly familiar and known. This change of residence resulted in my daily energy soaring with the abundance of green grass, small lakes, and fresh air. I was also able to fly my two cats to Paris since I now had a bigger living space with a highly-rare private garden. As I followed the strong energy pulling me forward, favorable opportunities opened up because my energy resonated with what I was ready to manifest next. It was in hindsight that I realized the past life connections to this region of France and why it felt like home.

As a Trapeze Artist voyages on in her spiritual growth journey with higher levels of self-trust, inspiring possibilities, supportive allies by her side, and past life connections revealing themselves, the perfect life can line up quickly based on her energy, intention, and consciousness. She is now ready to experience the highest possible heights.

6.
FINDING TOP

A TRAPEZE ARTIST HAS seen visuals of God being above her everywhere: in church, on buildings, in movies, in her meditations. She looks up for guidance. She looks up to find a higher perspective, a greater understanding, a knowing truth. She looks up with awe at a proud oak tree, a glorious monument, a historical statue, a seemingly impossible skyscraper. She looks up to a respected CEO, her cherished parents, a wise teacher. She looks up for the light of the sun, the sparkle of the stars, the glow of the moon. She looks up for inspiration, hope, and to witness prayers dancing in Notre Dame. She looks up.

In the area of spiritual growth, the "top" can show up as unhealthy displays of righteousness, all-knowing answers, and a one-size-fits-all perspective. This is the domain of cult leaders, gurus, and extremists, although it can also be the energy of respectful listeners, open curiosity, and compassionate leaders.

The perception of being at the "top" is a perspective held by the Ego-Mind and the Elevator, which are fueled by Earth Consciousness's favorite qualities: achievement, status, and recognition. Her human Self recognizes this perspective of being at the top, and loves it! What a beautiful thing to feel a sense of accomplishment, to know herself as powerful and successful! She has earned it all with her actions. None of these sensations should be minimized or negated or denied to her. She surely deserves the rewards, emotional highs, social recognition, and inner power of being here; it is all intoxicatingly delicious.

Yet the Soul and the Spiral do not have this same perspective of achievement and success. A Trapeze Artist is always exactly where she needs to be, and yes, some places along the way feel more rewarding and uplifting than others. To the Soul, the value of being at the "top" is the same value as being at the bottom if she is willing to expand her consciousness to see the gifts at both end of the spectrum. There is beauty in the growing and beauty in the having; strength in lack and strength in obtaining. The Soul finds the growth in every scenario. It is a continual supporter of what she is ready to learn at this phase of the journey. And the Soul knows that she is always Love, and Success, and Perfection, and the stars, and the skyscrapers wherever she goes.

So when a Trapeze Artist is at the "top" of her

journey, she feels she is finally at a higher version of herself. She feels closer to Divine energy than ever before. This pinnacle is the peak and the goal and the finish line. Everything has lined up properly for her success. Now she is at the same altitude as the stars and the statues and the skyscrapers. She has arrived, she's there, she did it! This is what it's all been about, right?

But the journey is far from over.

Up to this point, a Trapeze Artist has been living with her eyes on a prize, her sights set on the mountaintop. And now she's here. So she shifts her energy from achieving to maintaining as a ploy to not let go of her grasp on this well-earned dream. She has put so much into obtaining this pinnacle that she can't even imagine her path going anywhere else. No way. Not an option. Not even a possibility to consider.

Yet her wise Soul has a more valuable and powerful plan to offer her.

It is now time for a Trapeze Artist to meet her greatest fear.

7.
SURRENDER AND SUPREME SEPARATION FROM GOD

ENERGY IS ALWAYS IN motion. Change is a guarantee as the journey of spiritual growth unfolds. Energy changes will occur and each one will offer a Trapeze Artist new levels of enlightenment. But her perception of the changes may be disheartening in the moment when she has lost her grasp, or can't maintain her position, or loses what she has worked so hard to obtain. She is in shock. Disbelieving. Questioning. Stunned.

The Ego-Mind readily rushes in to provide the verdict of failure. A fall from grace, a demotion, a failure to be successful. She may go to a place where it feels personal, or she questions her self-worth, or she doubts herself. She may look back on everything she did and try to determine if she did something wrong, or didn't do something perfectly, or if she forgot something and should go back to redo it and just start again. No matter where her energy spins, her Ego-Mind just keeps telling her it all amounts to falling down the Elevator shaft.

Externally, these changes may appear to be a relationship ending, divorce, job loss, financial crisis, friendships leaving, moving residence, personal breakdown, and/or a significant life loss. This is when a Trapeze Artist feels a crushing blow to what she has obtained, where she has put her value, her energy, her identity. She was at the top and now she is not. She had the dream and now she does not.

But in her heart of hearts, in the same place where her Soul whispers to her and she experiences peace, a Trapeze Artist knows what is happening. *She knows.* She's just not ready to go there yet and consciously acknowledge it. So she holds the Truth of what is happening as far away from her energy as possible, arms straight out in front to shield it from arriving closer. She fights to keep the approaching circumstances away, away, away. She is resisting the next stage of her journey.

She is fighting the Surrender.

Surrender is the most challenging experience for a Trapeze Artist's inner warrior. She grew up learning all about ambition and goals and how to climb the ladder. She has learned to overcome, to speak up for herself, to go for what she wants, and to not settle for anything, anywhere. She has been trained to *keep trying* and *think outside the box* and to tap into her inner Scarlet O'Hara: "After all, tomorrow is another day!"

Interestingly, her unconscious perception of herself and her ability to surrender is limited because if she were to look more deeply into her life, she would realize she is actually incredibly amazing at surrender. She does it all the time.

Every night, she releases daily energies and her to-do list while exfoliating her face with care. She surrenders what she completed and washes away current cares, allowing the hours of the day to end.

During every phase of her life, she has surrendered one self-identity to expand into the next one. She surrendered her pre-pubescent Self to her emerging woman Self; her high school Self to her college Self; her intern Self to her empire-building Self. She has always released what was outgrown and outdated for a new, fresh, clean version of herself in the Now.

However, upon reflection, those instances of surrender felt different because they were planned, or expected, or chosen on some level. She knew they were coming, just as she knew the clock would strike 10 p.m. and the day would end. She was ready, prepared, willing and able to make those transitions as necessary. But this time, nothing was planned, or expected, or chosen, or even welcomed by her to experience this level of surrender.

Or was it?

From the perspective of Awakening Consciousness, the experience of surrender happens when it is perfectly needed. At this stage of the journey, her Soul is guiding her to release more unconscious energies, limiting belief systems, and relationships that she is now ready to move beyond. She has grown so much within the current experience that she is moving into another area of her Soul's growth. In order for that to happen, she has to let *this* go so another version can be created that reflects her expanding energy now.

Soul Contracts, Karmic Relationships, and Soul Mate connections may be complete due to the growth that has occurred. In *The Art of Trapeze*, this is when my relationship with Turhan ended because our energy was no longer in alignment. The Soul Contract, on my side, was to trust myself more and to honor what was best for my path. Feelings are a powerful messenger of that truth. A part of me knew the relationship was complete because I felt uncomfortable and that things were off between us. Our energies were no longer in sync. Yet I fought these messages through my Ego-Mind's desire to hold on, try more, make it work, and hang in there, because I loved him and valued our time together. It reached the point where I was staying in the relationship because I didn't want to lose it, either. When the Ego-Mind is running the show, we can try to avoid exactly what is needed next for our growth. On a Soul level, this is honored. Any choice is acceptable because there is value in all choices. But Soul Contracts make things messier because of the intensity of emotions involved, and even the unconscious roles we play within the connection. I was avoiding the surrender of the relationship to avoid the loss, the hurt, the pain of saying goodbye.

Surrender is a running undercurrent throughout *The Art of Trapeze*. Upon arriving in Paris, I surrendered one expectation of finding an apartment and opened up my intention so a bigger energy could guide me to a perfect home that benefited everyone involved. When I was offered two opportunities to work at two different U.S. Embassies, I surrendered having to figure it all out and trusted that the perfect solution would present itself. When my precious little Kitty ran away in my French village, and I felt heartbroken after doing everything I could to find her for 22 nights in a row, I finally surrendered to the feeling of loss I was trying oh-so-desperately to avoid. And when I reached the top of my dream in Paris, I fought as hard as I could to maintain everything I had created, even when it was clear an unstoppable force of change was steering me elsewhere. Then I finally made the courageous choice to surrender to not knowing what comes next which felt dreadful because, once again, *I didn't know what I didn't know.* I thought *that* version of my life was the main goal, but it turned out that something bigger was unfolding behind the scenes.

A Trapeze Artist has changed greatly and deeply up to this point on her spiritual journey. Not everything is meant to go forward and not everything has long-term value. On a Soul level, her learning is complete within that energetic experience, but only her Soul has that understanding at the time. Her human Self is fighting to hold on to the reality she has created because it is what she thought the Call of her Soul intended. Wasn't creating the dream all about having this relationship, job, idea, business, level of success?

Nope. For the Soul, there is a much grander experience underway than any one version of reality.

A Trapeze Artist may even wonder, SO WHAT about the surrender. Just do it. Let it all go. Start fresh, begin anew. Why is the surrender such a big deal? Get over it, move on, something else will happen next. No worries. It will all be okay. *I will land on my feet like I always do.*

But it's not just that. It's not just about giving herself a simple pep-talk and decadent glass of wine to find her confidence. There is more lurking underneath the surface, under the Ego-Mind's desire to control, under the knowingness that she'll figure it out. She knows a deeper terror lingers in the darkness. *She knows.* It's because the depths of surrender ultimately lead to her greatest unconscious fear: a supreme separation from God.

Just as being at the top felt like she was close to God's presence, surrendering feels like a plummeting fall away from Source energy. A disconnection from being seen, or heard, or acknowledged for who she really is, for what her energy and power really are.

Surrendering her unconscious Self can feel like a Dark Night of the Soul because a Trapeze Artist is required to let go of all control and previous self-definitions rooted in unconscious energies. *Who am I? What is my value? What am I connected to?* Her inner world will most likely move between her Ego-Mind's perspective and her Soul's perspective. She duels with the feelings of death, tragedy, hardship, and self-judgment, alongside her Soul's understanding that she is balancing energy, releasing what no longer serves her, learning more about her conscious power, and that she is always - always - connected to the eternal Spiral of Source energy. She just can't see or validate it outside of herself. She is being given the opportunity to own more of her ability to powerfully create her life. This is the real intense stuff and not everyone chooses it. Many run away in fear, or grab onto what they can control, follow an addiction, or return to what they know.

The emotional experience feels even bigger, fuller, and more overwhelming than she could have anticipated. *Why? Why does it all feel so BIG and emotionally pivotal, gut-wrenching, exhausting? What's the deal?* Even her brilliant mind feels stumped.

So she throws her head back to look up for hope, guidance, inspiration. She looks up.

And then she hears an unexpected answer with Divine clarity:

This feels emotionally big, dear one, because you are

energetically experiencing every time, across all lifetimes, where you have felt a supreme separation from God.

A lightning bolt of calm runs through her being, soothing her questions with this wise insight.

My time in North Carolina included a brief experience of depression. And you better believe my Ego-Mind fought against sharing that experience! But when I trusted that experience was a crucial part of the story, it flowed out of me and offered many gifts about that growing time in my life. I was separated from my loved ones, had difficulty connecting with new friends, unexpectedly struggled with college classes, and lived by myself in a dark apartment. In all areas of my life, I felt separate and solitary, as I moved through a jolting emotional ride that brought me to the deepest, darkest parts of myself. Unbeknownst to my 21-year-old Self at the time, I was reliving past life energies that were not only about "right now" or current choices or "this situation." I had been guided to move to North Carolina for reasons I couldn't understand at the time, yet I had a knowingness that I was meant to be there. And it was all Divinely perfect.

It was only years later that I connected with my spiritual understanding of depression, which was my manifestation of a supreme separation from God. On a Soul level, I chose that experience to clear out those emotions and have the illusion of spiritual separation as a point of reference. The experience was real, but the perspective was an illusion because there is no way we can be separate from God energy; we are God energy. But the Ego-Mind can create the perspective of separation as a representation of its greatest fear around death. The experience of emotional surrender gifted me with the opportunity to clear out those fears, across all lifetimes, for myself. I became stronger within after this Dark Night of the Soul by owning everything I experienced at that time in my life as a gorgeous gift. Awakening Consciousness offers this understanding about the Soul's desire to choose lessons that support Soul growth, yet it may come up against the powerful inner programming of Earth Consciousness and Separation Consciousness.

Surrender has the power to drop a Trapeze Artist right down to the despairs of Separation Consciousness where her Ego-Mind sits on the throne. Surrender may feel like a point of weakness, or a version of failure, or a time of loss. Surrender strips a Trapeze Artist raw of layers of unconscious emotions, energies, and limitations.

But if she can find a quiet moment to tap into the energy of the Spiral, she will feel openings to her true, conscious power that she didn't even know were there. She will see that she is releasing what is no longer needed for the path ahead, and now stepping more fully into her conscious power. It can feel like the most powerless time because when she lets go of *everything* she was and *everything* she has known, what could possibly be next? What could be better than the Call of her Soul she was following?

Perhaps the better question to ask is, Can she choose to trust that she is going somewhere even more valuable?

Her Soul whispers back: *The best is yet to come.*

8.
OWNING HER CONSCIOUS PERSONAL POWER

THERE ARE NO SHORTCUTS at this point of the journey. The only way ahead is to go through all of the emotions, the fears, the doubts, *the stuff* that is right in front of her as a result of surrendering. And on some level, a Trapeze Artist wouldn't have it any other way because she knows she can do this. She IS this strong. She IS this brave. She IS this powerful and determined and courageous. She loves herself enough to show up and listen to her guidance, her Soul's whispers. Living authentically with brutal self-honesty is a commitment she has made to herself numerous times throughout the journey. She re-commitments to both her inner knowingness and her trust in something bigger than herself. *She's got this*.

Sure, some people may cop out at this point and circle back around to "Love, Light and Bliss! Think happy thoughts! Say those affirmations loudly and proudly! Smile and put on a happy face!" And sure, her Ego-Mind will want to prevent any type of vulnerability from being shown, or for her to look like a fool, or to be perceived as a failure. The Ego-Mind fears death, after all, so it is only trying to keep her safe. So she consciously sends the loud and proud Ego-Mind lots of Love and willingly connects to her Soul's wisdom because death is actually necessary at this time. It is required.

The death of her former life, or the relationship, or the dream, or that phase in her life, will be shocking. The unexpected feelings may be overwhelming. The realization of all she has become on the journey and yet no longer has in her life may hit her hard and fast, destabilizing what she has relied on. Soul Contracts end, job titles end, a change of residence occurs, her fears come up. A part of her dies. She is grieving the loss of her Unconscious Self. Grieving *who she was* in order to prepare for the birth of *who she truly is.*

And to add more weight to the mourning process, she is also ending everything she has learned and gained across all lifetimes that connect to this energetic experience.

As she surrenders her Unconscious Self, a Trapeze Artist reflects on everything - *everything* - she has experienced since she answered the Call of her Soul. She remembers earlier times on the journey when she feared all was lost, or over, or misguided. And was that ever true? Was she ever alone and lost and off-track? No. Never. She may feel all alone during this phase, but that solitude is essential. She must feel alone to feel her inner strength. She must have the experience of being *in it* because it is the only way she will see herself *through it* to the other side. She must be in her own energy to find her own answers and hear her own Soul's guidance. She must look up and look within.

At this time, when she is releasing and surrendering, Spirit will dance and sing and nurture and guide her on with angelic presence. Spirit will show her resources, teachers, and nurturing moments of peace that affirm the wisdom of her surrender. She will be given little joys and unexpected opportunities along the way to coax her forward with love and reassurance.

Leaving Paris was a significant surrender for me, and as I moved through it, I received numerous signs of Divine support. Unexpected money arrived in the mail to help ease my financial fears. My five pieces of Crazy-Bags luggage were all shipped for free on an international flight, even after I diligently researched quotes and thought I would pay a minimum of $750 bucks. And I was unexpectedly upgraded to a free first class seat on my international flight home as confirmation that I was moving forward in the right direction. The signs and confirmations were calming to my mind and heart that this was what I needed to do, as if my Soul was right there at the helm, flying the plane home.

At this point in the journey, a Trapeze Artist makes a powerful choice to return back to herself. The voice of her Conscious Self grows louder in her mind. She is actually awakening to more of her Soul energy, life purpose, supreme gifts, and above all else, her conscious power.

In the quiet moments, insights arise around everything she has experienced, and realizations hit her about all of the amazing things she's created with her energy. Choices around relationships, emotional patterns, and belief systems all come to light. Or, more accurately, come up to her conscious light. She begins to see how her energy was always present in all areas of her life. If she manifested a significant Soul Contract based on energetic alignment, then she also manifested the completion of it perfectly. If she created wonderful professional opportunities or recognition or a raise or a fabulous new position, then she also created what developed afterwards when the energy changed. If she connected with something for her best and highest good, then she also disconnected from it for her best and highest good. *Everything she created with her powerful energy has always been for her best and highest good.*

A Trapeze Artist sees how her power was within her every step of the way, and how taking responsibility for her energy fuels her up instantly. She created everything about her story. *Everything.* Of course it's easier to take ownership of the awesome manifestations and wonderful developments, but her energetic power is always on. She sees the power in the learning, growth, and Self-understanding in all areas and ways.

If I didn't create all aspects of my life, then who did?

Her Soul smiles. Then it whispers back, *When you're alive, you're in lesson.*

Awakening Consciousness provides room for her to ask even more powerful questions: *Why did I manifest this experience? What are the highest understandings for me to learn? What is the best way to move forward now?*

She begins to see that a special blend of energies contributed to all experiences, including past life energies, Soul Contracts, karmic patterns, and her unconscious belief systems. The full story is bigger than right now, this lifetime, this one journey, this calendar year. It is only one place on the Soul's Spiral, after all. But for the first time she can see it clearly and brightly. Her energy is so incredibly big; bigger than she could have imagined when she was at the "top." There was no way she could have seen this energy within Separation Consciousness or Earth Consciousness. It is only within Awakening Consciousness that she understands how vast and limitless her possibilities are. Simply breathtaking.

She claims responsibility for her experiences in every way, even if she doesn't know the *why*, or *how*, or *when*. Her Ego-Mind will pop in with those inquiries, of course. She will consciously focus her attention on transmuting emotional, physical, mental, and psychological energies to higher expressions through bodywork, meditation, spiritual practices, and conscious choices. A Trapeze Artist will continually let go, remove, complete, and release parts of her experience that do not support her power and Self-Love. She has arrived at a new place of knowing herself. Awakening Consciousness has brought her to levels of Self-Love, Peace, Forgiveness, Gratitude, and Joy.

And now it is time for her Conscious Self to return back to the Unconscious World.

Yikes.

9.
BEING CONSCIOUS IN AN
UNCONSCIOUS WORLD

A TRAPEZE ARTIST RETURNS to life in the Unconscious World as a completely new version of herself. She is significantly, irrevocably changed. An inner makeover, a huge transformation, a reconstruction of Self has occurred. She no longer recognizes the woman who originally left to answer the Call of her Soul. She realizes more about who she is energetically and spiritually. She sees what she never knew was there. And she didn't even realize how unconscious she had been in the Unconscious World.

Now she feels like a total misfit. She is no longer a citizen of the status quo, and the feeling of being an imposter, an outsider silently weighs on her. Culture shock may figure prominently in this stage because she is seeing everything around her with new eyes, a fresh perspective. As she tries to adjust back into the Unconscious World, she faces an internal dark force in the form of her Ego-Mind telling her to fit back in. *Just do what you've done before. Don't make this so hard on yourself. You're not that special or better than anyone else.* The desire to participate in the Unconscious World is seductive because it can feel comfortable and safe. The desire to do and say "all the right things" may even be an automatic reflex because adjusting back into the Unconscious World is foreign territory to navigate. She cannot go back to who she was and she doesn't want to pretend to be less than her Conscious Self. Her commitment to her own growth is too strong, too driving, to abandon. As a result, new challenges arise.

Relationships change and friendships end. She has little in common with long-time friends, and more impatience around unconsciousness in general. She will probably not connect as well with people who have not experienced a Dark Night of the Soul; or those who do not know the true energies of surrender and trust; or people who have never answered the Call of her Soul. A Trapeze Artist may feel sassy, feisty, impatient when listening to them complain about a relationship, or an unhappy job, or a lack of money, or anything that signifies Separation Consciousness. She may feel the need to sit on her hands just to make sure she doesn't slap someone silly for complaining about what they're creating in their life.

In these moments when she is triggered, she has

an opportunity to make the choice to open up to Heart Consciousness and find a connection between herself and Them. If she can release the annoyance, or anger, or impatience, she will recognize how she was exactly the same way when she was Unconscious. She will recognize the common phrases, and thoughts, and questions, and perceptions that she once held, too. She will be able to see a previous version of herself in Them. And how would she want to be treated if she only knew how to operate within Separation Consciousness and Earth Consciousness? This is not about pity, or being better than Them, or taking on the responsibility of another's path. It is about finding the meeting points between herself and Them with detachment, acceptance, and respect. *They don't know what they don't know. I've been there, too.*

So she listens with an open heart, and after discerning if it is worth her energy and time, a Trapeze Artist may gently say, "Ya know, I've come to look at life really differently after my recent experiences and have a new view around these types of things. Are you interested in hearing another potential way to understand this scenario?"

Even if they kindly listen to her perspective, and don't get it, or don't care at all, she knows that each person understands everything based on their best choices and in their own way. The Spiral honors every place for everyone. And many people will not answer a Call of their Soul in their lifetime. This is perfect. This is a Soul choice to be honored. Every

Soul chooses what is best for them, on their own timeline, at their own pace, in their own manner. She sees that each person is on their own Spiral. No judgment, no requirements, nothing is wrong. All is in Divine order at all times.

However, this realization will motivate her to seek out others who have also answered the Call of their Soul. She will look for a tribe, a support group, some select allies who *get it* the same way she does. This may be a very small circle of people, or it may be no one. She may even feel herself slipping into Separation Consciousness for a bit due to the loneliness of this phase, but she doesn't fear it because she knows she has the power to rise to Awakening Consciousness when she's ready. She can handle ongoing adjustments as she ventures forth. *I've got this.*

During this stage, a Trapeze Artist needs to call on her wisdom, discernment, and boundaries more often. She needs to be extra careful about how she spends her energy, what she commits to, and whom she engages with to ensure she is always self-honoring and full of self-Love for who she is now. She has realized who she no longer is and is not quite sure where she fits in yet. Or if she WANTS to fit in because it would limit her authentic expression.

She has come way too far on her spiritual growth journey to revert back now. But there must be a way to proceed ahead in the Unconscious World with her Conscious Self. Or else what has been the point of this journey?

10.
AWAKENING TO DEEPER SOUL POWER

A TRAPEZE ARTIST STOPS to take a breath and look around. Readjusting back into the Unconscious World has brought up more *stuff* than she expected. It was not the smooth, easy transition she had hoped for. In fact, it was not the return she wanted at all because it has revealed more *stuff* hiding underneath the surface that she, in all her shiny, new Conscious Self glory, wasn't even aware was there. And that's exactly the point of this stage.

The purpose of integrating her Conscious Self with the Unconscious World is to reveal any lingering aspects of her inner world that she hasn't seen yet. In other words, the Unconscious World will bring her face-to-face with more of her own Shadow Self. It is her Shadow, out of sight, dwelling in the background, that is still working within her energy field and preventing her from moving forward as her Conscious Self.

Her Shadow Self will show her more areas where she has unconsciously given her power away: to others' opinions, thoughts, ideals, institutions, family members, expectations, needs.

Her Shadow Self will reveal more ways she has previously sabotaged her own efforts due to deep fears. It will show where she has a repetitive, limiting life theme that is finally ready to be changed.

Her Shadow Self will show her the previous times when she gave up on herself, or turned away from her inner knowing, or didn't believe in the vastness of her dreams, or didn't think she was worth it.

Her Shadow Self will reveal where she projects *anything* onto another so she does not have to claim responsibility for it. She will see more truth around her unconscious reactions, inner dialogue, hidden emotions, and limiting beliefs than ever before. Her Shadow Self will bring up any variety of energies that she denied, or ignored, or only saw in another. And it could feel brutal.

A deeper purification is now required. Just as she did when she initially answered the Call of her Soul, a Trapeze Artist goes within again to consciously determine the source of her Shadow Self and then transmute the lower vibrating energies into what she wants to create next. *What is her next dream? If she could have anything right now, what would it be? Knowing she can consciously create anything, how does she want to feel and live on a daily basis?*

The intensities around this experience are beyond what is happening in the present. *The deeper purification is that she is doing the work across all lifetimes.* She is realizing her Soul's themes, lessons, healing, and growth across multiple lives that are happening in parallel lifetimes. This is when she gets to the heart of the wound and the source of her Shadow Self that has existed across all experiences of time and space. Examining the root themes and lessons of Soul Contracts, Karmic Relationships, and Soul Mates often play a figurative role in this process. If she doesn't examine these energies, they will continue to present themselves in unconscious ways.

The purification phase may be two weeks, two months, two years depending on what is right for her. It is a personal, sacred time of going into the depths of her being, and it can feel like another death, another stripping away of her self-identity. But it will lead to new revelations about her Soul's story.

I intentionally left out two years of my story in *The Art of Trapeze* because that was my purification time. I was back in the Unconscious World as a more powerful version of myself, and I needed time to figure out what I wanted next, to become comfortable in my new skin. I focused on spiritual learning, studying, and following my expanding interests. I did share some of my experiences in the book, including physical energetic clearings through Qigong, Jin Shin Jyutsu, body cleanses, exercising, and meditation. I also found acupuncture effective and many glimpses of my spiritual team during these clearings and openings. Spiritually, I consulted trusted sources for astrology sessions, intuitive readings, past life regressions, Akashic Record readings, energy healing, and a slew of spiritual books. With each energetic release, I became clearer about what I wanted to create next, and what I did NOT want to experience. I grew to understand more about my energetic imprint, my soul purpose, and where to direct my energy for the highest levels of joy, success, and fulfillment. Have you ever experienced a purification of an older version of yourself?

I would love to proudly declare that this process was linear, fast, and obvious; it wasn't. Not a bit. This stage of the journey was messy at times; foggy and confusing at others. Some days I even hated it and resisted it. But regardless of what occurred, or did not occur, I made a continual commitment to trust myself. I returned to that place of deep knowingness, that sacred place we all possess, that is the energy of our Soul. I knew I was alive for Divine reasons and even through the yucky, mucky, boring days, I am connected to the All That Is. Some days, this mentality is what sustained me when nothing was occurring on my preferred timeline.

Purification can happen for a Trapeze Artist on all levels: physically, emotionally, psychologically, mentally, spiritually, energetically. Like cleaning out the closest, she tosses everything out and then carefully chooses what to bring back in. She is integrating the needs, fears, and lower energies of her Ego-Mind with the full, unconditional love of her Soul. She is turning her Shadow Self into greater light, giving more love to her greater fears.

With her conscious power, a Trapeze Artist chooses to clear out any and all remaining Unconscious energies that no longer serve her highest and best good. Self-sabotage? Done. Remaining small in her energy? Over. Limiting what she thinks she can have in a partner? Finished. Downplaying the figures she should see on a paycheck? Gone.

The ultimate gift of this time is the deeper awakening to Cosmic Consciousness. She detaches from the perspective of this lifetime, this journey, this place, and opens up to herself as an eternal energy filled with unlimited potentials. The wisdom of Cosmic Consciousness floods into her psyche as she opens up to herself as a timeless energy connected to everything, everyone, every potential. Anything she wants to create and do next is possible.

In *The Art of Trapeze*, I reference *The Awakening* by Kate Chopin because of its timeless wisdom about expanding beyond the societal roles we play and the unconscious self-definitions we accept about our place in the world. Cosmic Consciousness accelerates us beyond the "here and now" perspective and catalyzes us forward into unlimited options around how to share and exert one's Soul energy in the physical world. When all illusions of constraints are removed, she can intentionally imprint her energy in the world in a manner that honors the fullness of who she is without labels, roles, titles, or a clever brand name.

The next part of her spiritual growth journey may not be clear, but she can feel the energy of expansion guiding her forward. She has absorbed higher spiritual knowledge. She is new, yet again, and her energy feels even clearer, even brighter, than ever before. After everything she has experienced, and felt, and known, and realized, and purified, there must be a useful purpose for it all. There must be a point to all of these stages.

But what is it?

She looks up for understanding. She looks within for peace.

And then a new whisper arrives from her Soul.

It is a whisper lined in gold and laced with Love.

11.
MASTERY OF HER CONSCIOUSNESS

SHE LISTENS INTENTLY AND gets it.
She gets it.
She gets it.
Her Soul whispers loudly:

You are ALL types of consciousness.

You are every form of energy and all expressions of it.

There is not only one type of consciousness to embody; there are all types to make the most of your energy.

And you will continually move through all energies as long as you are in your glorious human body.

The Call of her Soul was not about a single dream, or destination, or goal. *It was never about Paris, dear one.*

The Call of her Soul was an awakening to all that she is with no limitations, no self-judgments, no overactive Ego-Mind, no Shadow, no restrictions.

Answering the Call of her Soul allowed her to go into ALL depths of her energy. She went to the deepest fears and the tallest achievements; the widest expressions and the narrowest interpretations. She experienced unconscious energies within herself that she has carried for lifetimes. She dove into her fears of supreme separation. She soared up to her grandest manifestations. She cleared Soul Contracts, Karmic Relationships, and her Shadow Self, and transmuted them all into greater light. She is the eternal energy of the Spiral. She is also the physical presence of the Elevator. She is all types of consciousness in their perfection and grace. She recognizes how ALL of her Self, her experiences, her energies are valuable. She is All That Is.

With Mastery of her Consciousness, a Trapeze Artist understands that Separation Consciousness will still show up on her spiritual journey, but it is not to be judged. Experiences of grief will unfold, whether they are triggered by the loss of a parent, or saying goodbye to a pet, or the ending of an important relationship. She may experience temporary sadness, or financial fears, or doubts about her abilities, but she knows she can always choose to release those fears of separation she has known across lifetimes. Those fears aren't really her. Then she will consciously choose what energy to connect with next.

She knows that Earth Consciousness is the gift of

being in a physical body on a gorgeous planet. She chooses to connect with the joys of daily life and the delights of her senses. Her intelligent mind is an asset and her Ego-Mind is an ally. She can make the most of her surroundings at all times and enjoy the highs of materials success, hard work, and achievement. It is all available to her as a slice of the spiritual pie.

She feels how Heart Consciousness motivates her to connect with other people in an honest, authentic practice. She can choose to give of her time, money, ideas, and energy, and receive from others in the same way. She can Forgive regularly, Love often, and be Compassion in action. She can go within to dance in the wonders of Peace and then offer that energy back to her world. She can activate Joy daily, at any time.

She celebrates Awakening Consciousness as it opens her up to the power of her conscious choices, Soul wisdom, and responsibility for her energy. She embraces all of her potentials, especially the opportunities to upgrade limiting behaviors, patterns, and belief systems. She understands the power of detachment, the importance of acceptance, and the necessity of discernment. She views every being as a fellow traveler, a powerful Soul. She sends them energetic high-fives and silently salutes them with a respectful *Namaste*.

She absorbs the high-vibrations of Cosmic Consciousness as a reminder that she is always supremely connected to the eternal energies of the

Universe. She is a vital, needed component of conscious energy on the planet now. And she is guided to offer, shine, and BE that light in the best possible ways.

But it is not only about her.

The understandings, connections, and wisdom she has connected with at this stage in her spiritual growth now offer another important insight.

The journey is for All.

Mastery occurs when a Trapeze Artist makes the connection that the Call of her Soul and all of her spiritual growth experiences can be offered back to humanity as wisdom, as an offering, as a contribution to the planet through unlimited means. A gift of service, of words, of energy, of action, of prayer; the gift is uniquely hers to determine, create, and share. How can she consciously uplift, up-light, upgrade the world around her? (High heels optional.)

At this stage, a Trapeze Artist owns the fullness of her energy, all of her experiences, and the unlimited opportunities she has to be higher consciousness in the world. Just her energetic Beingness is a valuable contribution to the planet.

New types of Soul Contracts, Soul Mates, Soul Groups, and lessons will arrive in this energy. Her growth will continue on as new opportunities to learn, important allies, deep emotions, and incredible manifestations will appear. *When you're alive, you're in lesson.*

One type of relationship manifestations at this

stage are Kindred Spirits. Once she has completed important Soul lessons, a Trapeze Artist graduates to another experience of partnership and relationships that are composed of higher energies, such as trust, abundance, joy, laughter, and peace. Kindred Spirit connections do not contain karmic energies, emotional wounds, or deep healing lessons. These relationships have greater flow, ease, and a lightness to them that was not present or available while completing key Soul Contracts and moving through intense Soul growth. Kindred Spirits may have past life experiences together, but they were not tangled up in healing wounds or intense emotional themes. Imagine a Kindred Spirit as the person on the sidelines watching the game and not participating on the field. A Kindred Spirit often arrives after deep energetic clearings have occurred. A whole new type of relationship experience is created that could feel "too good to be true." This is the energetic connection I felt immediately with Jay in *The Art of Trapeze*. We had an ease with one another because we did not need to experience deep healing together. We were united through a Kindred Spirit connection. And now he is my husband.

Another essential component of Mastery is the need to detach from multiple interpretations around her spiritual growth journey. Not everyone will understand it, or get it, or have a similar life experience to relate to. A Trapeze Artist will experience a variety of perspectives about her journey, and each bit of feedback will depend on the consciousness filter of that person.

The filter of Separation Consciousness says, "Oh no, it didn't last! She experienced struggle, hurdles, loss, and it all fell apart. That sucks."

The filter of Earth Consciousness asserts, "She achieved a lot and reached some great milestones and goals, good for her. Time to get up and try for more success!"

Heart Consciousness offers, "She had an amazing journey filled with love, forgiveness, joy, growth, and personal growth. How heart-warming and inspiring!"

Awakening Consciousness shares, "Look at all she created for her Soul's growth! Wow, she completed cycles of behaviors, released big energies, understood her lessons, and connected with more of her power."

Cosmic Consciousness beams, "Her growth is connected to my growth, which is connected to our growth, and the overlaps move us all forward together. We are all Souls experiencing this human journey together. Namaste, Soul sister."

Mastery will remind her that she has the bandwidth to understand the variety in responses. All is in Divine order. Each person's response reflects where they are in their growth, and from the Spiral's perspective, it is always perfect. Everyone is exactly where they need to be.

As a Master of her own consciousness, she also understands that anything that triggers her now is merely a reflection of an unconscious fear she holds within that is being reflected back to her. If someone judges her journey and that judgment triggers her on some level, it is because she is unconsciously judging her journey in the same way as well. It is easier to project the reaction onto another person instead of owning it as part of her Shadow Self creeping back in for attention. Or else it wouldn't bother her.

The Spiral continues up. Her spiritual growth journey has reached a higher point, and the energy keeps going, keeps evolving. A new beginning is near. A new Call of her Soul will be answered. (Her Soul has her digits on auto-dial, after all.) The next Call of her Soul will be within a different energy field of possibilities and potentials. There will be more to learn, and understand, and feel, and master. She knows she can handle it because she is more comfortable in her own Soul skin than ever before. And it pretty much rocks.

She takes a few deep breaths.

And waits for the clarity, knowingness, and calm to arrive.

When the next Call of her Soul finally comes through in the most perfect way, in the most perfect time, she is ready to once again say YES.

Then a Trapeze Artist leaps to experience the thrills of another grand journey of consciousness.

12.
ESSENTIALS OF A SPIRITUAL GROWTH JOURNEY

A SPIRITUAL JOURNEY OF expanding consciousness is a choice. It is stepping away from one definition of Self and entering a whole new expansive version of your own energy. As the eleven stages just demonstrated, it is a heady combination of multiple experiences, breakthroughs, emotions, and personal understandings that are uniquely your own.

I mentioned at the beginning of this book that I have been through this journey four times without even knowing it was *a thing*. The glorious view of hindsight (and *maybe* a few glasses of wine) revealed how each time I answered the Call of my Soul it was to clear out energies, experiences, and karmic connections. Every journey was an opportunity to heal, learn, grow, and transform a part of myself *if I chose to do so*. It is notable to say that not every person wants to change themselves or do deep spiritual work. Again, it comes down to personal choice, interest, and what feels right for your energy.

A spiritual growth journey has numerous potentials, just as expanding consciousness can unfold in unlimited ways. Beautiful, amazing, perfect! So how do you know if you've completed a journey? Referencing Joseph Campbell's studies of mythology and folklore, he calls the three main segments of a journey the Departure, the Initiation, and the Return. In terms of spiritual growth, I refer to these three essential segments as the Opening, the Deepening, and the Renewal.

Each time I set off on a journey, I was operating within a certain type of consciousness that was applicable for my highest and best growth at that time, and every version held the three essential segments - the Opening, the Deepening, and the Renewal. Three of my journeys had a unique combination of the eleven stages we just explored. Answering the Call of my Soul to move to Paris was a comprehensive journey involving all eleven stages and all types of consciousness.

THE OPENING

The Unconscious Self answers a Call of the Soul to go beyond known bounds. Curiosity, a yearning, deep questions, a crisis, or any type of catalyst can spark the desire to spiritually explore and open up to know Self more. Spiritually, this can show up as leaving behind an organized religion, belief system, or spiritual understanding you've known your whole life in order to see what else may resonate with you. The overarching theme is the desire to leave *what is known* to venture forward and discover *what is not yet known*.

In terms of personal consciousness, there is an opening to spiritual topics, interests, concepts, studies, teachings, and philosophies. The desire to say "never mind!" and turn around is strong and seductive at some point because it may feel safe to return to a former version of Self. The choice to venture forward into unknown territory is required in this segment as a commitment to Soul discovery and personal energy. The journey unfolds with greater openings to Self and unseen assistance from spiritual energies, such as meeting your Spirit Guides and angels for the first time. The developments that happen at this time are in preparation for the Deepening.

The Opening segment of the journey can include all of these stages, or a combination of them:
- The Call of Her Soul
- Refusing Her Soul's Whispers
- Opening Up To A Greater Power

THE DEEPENING

Discomfort emerges as an inner battle brews around all energies being carried within, but new opportunities, exciting developments, and like-minded friends arrive, as well. This is the phase when new spiritual classes, teachers, healing modalities, and resources are explored. Questions come up, unconscious patterns are noticed, inner programming is challenged, and deep work is required. Personal Ego-Mind energies are examined. Soul Contracts, past life scenarios, Karmic Relationships and Soul Groups all show up to pull you into deeper understandings of your personal energies with the intention of shining light on unconsciousness.

Extremes are experienced, from exhausting emotional depths to the emergence of a deep inner knowingness. A Dark Night of the Soul occurs to purge and transform unconsciousness, which can signal a turning point in the spiritual growth journey. Your Shadow Self may appear at this time, or in the next segment, but it will also bring you gifts of greater consciousness. As clearing and purging occurs, new levels of conscious personal power form to carry you forward into a higher version of Self for the Renewal.

The Deepening of the journey can include all of

these stages, or a combination of them:
- Manifesting, Soul Contracts,
    Past Life Connections
- Finding Top
- Surrender and Supreme Separation From God
- Owning Her Conscious Personal Power

THE RENEWAL

The Renewal is a spiritual connection back to the pure essence of your Soul's energy. Much has been changed, realized, and altered that has formed a different version of Self. The journey may be uncomfortable and the desire to own your new energy will be strong.

After opening up to more of your Soul and learning about your energy deeply, you have more wisdom to offer and share than ever before. This doesn't mean everyone resonates with what you have to share, but the bigger picture is you're energetically contributing to humanity's knowledge base and providing more perspectives to choose from. Like a spiritual boomerang, the Renewal is about returning to the place you left with high vibrating intentions as a Master of your own Consciousness. It is important that whatever you choose to offer back resonates with your energy, even if it is simply meditating, shining your light, or being You in that environment. Not offering anything back to the world is a choice, but it keeps the spiritual growth journey personal instead of allowing others to learn from it, too.

In order for the journey to be complete, you need to come back to the place you left. Many times, on a spiritual quest, people leave for exploration and stay gone because they believe (or assume) they are done with *that*, the place they exited. Energetically, this is true as a part of their experience within that level of knowledge, understanding, or belief is complete. However, the point of a journey is that you bring wisdom, teachings, an offering, *something* back to share with everyone. Spiritual elitism shows up in those who don't believe they have to do anything with what they've learned.

The Renewal segment of the journey can include all of these stages, or a combination of them:
- Being Conscious In An Unconscious World
- Awakening To Deeper Soul Power
- Mastery of Her Consciousness

CHARACTERISTICS OF THE JOURNEY

I would love to say that each time I experienced a spiritual growth journey it was a neat and tidy path; linear and well-planned and oh yeah, *I know what comes next.* Nope, it's not. There are many unknown delights, new developments, and unexpected ways the journey unfolds. It happens on the best timeline for each person and it is uniquely their own Soul energy experience based on what they are ready to learn and understand. Each journey occurs according to a person's preferred pace, speed, comfort level, and commitment.

However, there are eight defining characteristics of the spiritual growth journey:

- **It's solo.** She does it by herself, for herself.
- **It's unknown.** She moves outside of a comfort zone.
- **It tests limits**. She is pushed by multiple external circumstances.
- **It's emotional.** She experiences the full spectrum of her inner world.
- **It's transformational.** She experiences a death, rebirth, and is forever changed.
- **It's risky.** She is required to leap somehow - emotionally, financially, psychologically, mentally, spiritually.
- **It's comprehensive.** She moves through most of the stages of the journey, and experiences the Opening, the Deepening, and the Renewal.
- **It's a permanent and significant change in self-identity.** She becomes more of herself than ever before.

So, why go on the journey? Why should a modern heroine answer the Call of her Soul in the first place? The only guarantee is she will experience deep, profound changes and nothing about herself will be the same afterward. As I've mentioned numerous times, it all comes down to personal choice, interest level, and a desire for spiritual growth. The rewards of a journey are difficult to quantify, and I'm still learning as I go, but I have identified numerous incentives, experiences, and life-transforming events that I had no way of knowing about before answering the Call of my Soul. A few reasons to embark on a journey of consciousness include moving away from unconscious Self limitations, expanding into the fullness of Soul love, experiencing the energy of the Spiral, and honing in on the importance of self-trust.

Other reasons why a modern heroine chooses a journey of consciousness is because she can.

Because she has amazing heaps of spiritual support.

Because she is alive to know herself as a limitless Soul.

Because she is awesomeness in three-inch heels.

Because she is the heroine of her own story.

FREQUENTLY ASKED QUESTIONS

Does every woman need to go on a journey to be more conscious in her life?

No. We each come in to our human experience with our individual Soul lessons and areas of growth to explore that may or may not involve consciousness. I do believe, however, that there is more support on the planet than ever before for this area of spiritual growth.

But there are no shortcuts. There are multiple ways to *attempt* to take shortcuts or "talk the talk" but not know the walk. Anyone can buy a brownie mix off the store shelf, add water, and bake it. That recipe will have one type of energy, and it will resonate with others in the same energy field. Or you can invest time and energy into creating your own recipe and know every ingredient deeply and personally, which will be another energetic creation. Some people may rush to an end result so they can have the title of "master" for a variety of intentions, but energy never lies – and there is NO end result! We are all in a continual process of mastering ourselves in physical form, and there is no mastery over others.

At the end of the day, you are only responsible for your own energy, your own consciousness, your own journey. Not everyone wants to do this work, and as I previously stated, there are no requirements to do so. But if you're curious and feel the nudge, I suggest trusting it.

I don't think moving to Paris is in the cards for me, but how do I experience my own journey of consciousness?

Whatever is calling to you to *do* is where to begin. That answer comes from you - and only from you - and opening up to receive insights is a beautiful place to begin. Listen to what you hear during meditations or within your own essence. Trust what feels right because the journey could be any number of choices that inspire you to grow: Weight loss. Healing deep family wounds. Opening up your own business. Raising kids at home. Examining your belief systems.

In terms of spiritual growth, follow the spiritual topics you are interested in and see what information resonates with you. A journey to deeper parts of your Soul's energy will be present in whatever you are guided to explore. You are here to find your own answers.

I believe every person knows what they need to do, or follow, or explore, but we look for validation, affirmation, justification from others that it is okay to go for it. No permission is needed outside of yourself to answer the Call of your Soul. Perhaps that is really what you're seeking to hear.

Are there astrological connections to the journey?

Yes! Astrologically, the journey is connected to the energy of Pluto, the 8th house, and the archetypal sign of Scorpio. A Pluto transit to a key part of your natal astrology chart signifies, among other things, deep transformational change. A Pluto conjunction to a personal planet (especially your Sun or Moon) or a conjunction to a chart angle (Ascendant, IC, Descendant, MC) is usually the most intense experience of the energy. Similar themes show up with connections to the 8th house and planets in Scorpio. A professional astrologer can assist you in understanding your chart, your natal energies, and what you are learning at this time. Evolutionary astrologers specialize in Plutonic energies and may be the best resource for questions about your Soul's journey.

This journey sounds very private and personal. I don't think other people in my life will understand it, and I don't even know if I'd want to share my spiritual growth with them (at least not yet). Can I do something on my own that is sacred and meaningful?

Yes! You have identified two key points about the aspects of a spiritual growth journey - personal and sacred. I offer a private course to support you through your own journey. I will be your guide and mentor, but the journey is all yours.

The private course will be available on SpiritualityUniversity.com in January 2014. Or stay in touch for updates on my website, **ConsciousCoolChic.com**

REFERENCES

Campbell, Joseph. *The Hero with a Thousand Faces*. 1st edition, Bollingen Foundation, 1949. 2nd edition, Princeton University Press. 3rd edition, New World Library, 2008.

Campbell, Joseph. *Pathways to Bliss: Mythology and Personal Transformation*. Edited by David Kudler. New World Library, 2004.

Moyers, Bill and Joseph Campbell. *The Power of Myth*. Anchor: Reissue edition, 1991.

Murdock, Maureen. *The Heroine's Journey: Woman's Quest For Wholeness*. Shambhala Publications, 1990.

Tom, Michael. *An Open Life: Joseph Campbell in Conversation with Michael Toms*. Harper Perennial, 1990.

Other Books by Molly McCord

Coming in 2014!
Book Three in The Awakening Consciousness Series

The Unlimited Sparks of A Bonfire
By Molly McCord

The grand journey of consciousness continues with an exciting travel adventure!

From the frostbite blizzards of Moscow and the warm tropical breezes of Hawaii, to an isolated dry barren desert in Africa, a quiet French village on the outskirts of civilization, and a bustling geisha house in Japan, get ready for an inspiring exploration of life-changing experiences.

The Unlimited Sparks of a Bonfire is filled with spiritual connections, passion, emotional depths, and unexpected wisdom to connect you more personally with greater Soul discovery.

Bestselling author and spiritual teacher Molly McCord, M.A., takes you even deeper into the understandings of your Soul's energy with Book Three in the Awakening Consciousness Series.

Book Three in The Awakening Consciousness Series

THE
UNLIMITED
SPARKS
OF A
BONFIRE

FROM THE BESTSELLING AUTHOR OF
THE ART OF TRAPEZE AND
THE MODERN HEROINE'S JOURNEY OF CONSCIOUSNESS

MOLLY McCORD

Book One in The Awakening Consciousness Series

Discover Molly's bestselling spiritual memoir:

The Art of Trapeze:
One Woman's Journey of Soaring, Surrendering, and Awakening
By Molly McCord

Hit #1 in 2 Amazon categories!

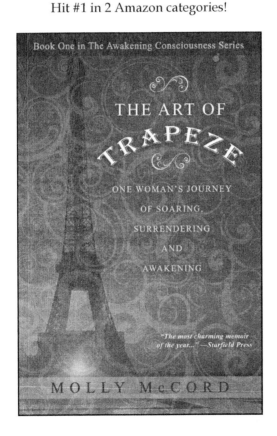

On a random Thursday morning, with nothing to lose and only a dream to gain, Molly McCord decides to move to Paris, France to follow the courageous call of her heart. She arrives in a city she has never visited before and where she knows no one, yet she trusts her ability to figure it out because her adventurous life has prepared her for this biggest of leaps. She carries the wisdom of Solitude, Strength, Style, Flexibility, Heart, Endurance, and Grace in her non-matching luggage collection.

Molly's soul-riveting experiences unfold in surprising ways as she discovers the joys and realities of life as a foreigner in France, falls in love with a sexy Turkish man, moves her cats across the Atlantic, enjoys the rare opportunity of working for a U.S. Ambassador, and creates the life of her dreams in less than two years.

Yet when unexpected developments require her to surrender once again, a higher consciousness catches her with a deeper spiritual awakening.

The Art of Trapeze soars with emotional honesty, delightful humor, unexpected wisdom, and inspiring spiritual perspectives around living life to the fullest when nothing is guaranteed except gravity.

"Beautifully written, charmingly funny - even hilarious - and remarkably open, honest, and down-to-earth, Ms. McCord has gifted us with a pure example of how life can be such a beautiful, grand adventure..." ~ Starfield Press

"In many ways, Molly tells you how to be brutally honest with your own soul and get on with your own life in an extremely courageous way." ~ Rick DiClemente, Author of *The Exquisite Zodiac*, Intuitive Astrologer

Conscious Thoughts:
Powerful Affirmations To Connect With
Your Soul's Language
By Molly McCord

This evolutionary guide is a rare combination of modern situations, past life connections, and powerful affirmations that speak to your Soul with high vibrational energy!

Affirmations are conscious thoughts that can be amazingly effective once the root energy is identified. Discover how to heal unconscious patterns, move beyond repetitive lessons, and change your understanding around what is holding you back in life.

Plus, get to the heart of how affirmations work,

why they support your spiritual growth, how to use them powerfully, what affirmations do NOT do, and six key tenets for maximum results.

The five short stories with past life connections and healing affirmations include:

Reclaiming Your Personal Power

Dealing With Shadow Feminine Energies

Adult Bullying

Your Body As Your Ally

Roadblocks to Creative Expression and A Loving Partnership

Enjoy over 40 original affirmations for Forgiveness, Love, Career, Health, Trust, Creativity, Prosperity, Living Your Best Life, and more!

Conscious Messages:
Spiritual Wisdom and Inspirations for Awakening
By Molly McCord

A practical, uplifting collection of high-vibrational messages to elevate your energy!

From affirming that Where You Are Is Where You Need to Be and owning your personal truth, to cosmic perspectives on emotional energy, being in alignment with your intentions, and expanding beyond limiting belief systems, these 21 channeled messages provide you with simple, direct perspectives about stepping more fully into your soul's light. One to keep on your nightstand for joy, clarity, and empowerment!

ABOUT THE AUTHOR

MOLLY McCORD, M.A., is a bestselling author and modern spiritual teacher with no religious affiliations. Her debut memoir, *The Art of Trapeze: One Woman's Journey of Soaring, Surrendering, and Awakening*, hit #1 in 2 Amazon categories within 3 days. She is published in *The Thought That Changed My Life Forever* alongside such luminaries as Dr. Michael Bernard Beckwith, Dr. Joe Dispenza, and Dr. Bernie Siegel.

The Art of Trapeze is Book One in **The Awakening Consciousness Series** which connects, for the first time, spiritual growth with Joseph Campbell's archetypal hero's journey. *The Modern Heroine's Journey of Consciousness* references the essential stages of spiritual growth. *The Unlimited Sparks of A Bonfire* (Spring 2014), Book Three in the Series, is a travel adventure that combines stories and spiritual information from the previous two books. Molly's other published books include *Conscious Messages: Spiritual Wisdom and Inspirations For Awakening* and *Conscious Thoughts: Powerful Affirmations To Connect With Your Soul's Language.*

Molly's popular website, ConsciousCoolChic.com was nominated by Intent.com for Best Spirituality Website in 2011. She is also a practicing intuitive astrologer, and has a popular weekly radio show that attracted over 70,000 downloads in the first year.

Molly lives in Seattle, WA with her husband.

Printed in Great Britain
by Amazon

35118670R00092